Treating Autism Today

Drawing together an international range of psychoanalytic practitioners, this collection provides a critique of mainstream models of autism, looking at the conceptual and ideological underpinnings of the behavioural and cognitive approaches popular today.

The first book to provide a psychoanalytic unpacking of standard non-analytic approaches, it offers a series of critical essays on mainstream assumptions, examining their history, foundations, and validity from a variety of angles. The authors consider, from the Lacanian perspective, the hypothesis of the biological-genetic causality of autism, as well as the claims of these approaches to offer effective therapy. These discussions are historically contextualised by an introduction and afterword that also provide pointers and references to further reading on Lacanian approaches to autism.

Illustrated throughout by clinical examples, *Treating Autism Today* will be of interest to Lacanian clinicians and scholars, as well as psychotherapists, psychologists, and those working with children diagnosed as being on the autistic spectrum.

Laura Tarsia is a psychoanalyst working with adults and young people in London. She is a member and lecturer at CFAR.

Kristina Valendinova is a psychoanalyst and translator in London and a member of CFAR and of the Cercle Freudien in Paris. She is the co-founder of Bubble and Speak, a "maison verte" drop-in for small children and their carers.

The Centre for Freudian Analysis and Research Library (CFAR)

Series Editors:
Anouchka Grose, Darian Leader, Alan Rowan

CFAR was founded in 1985 with the aim of developing Freudian and Lacanian psychoanalysis in the UK. Lacan's rereading and rethinking of Freud had been neglected in the Anglophone world, despite its important implications for the theory and practice of psychoanalysis. Today, this situation is changing, with a lively culture of training groups, seminars, conferences, and publications.

CFAR offers both introductory and advanced courses in psychoanalysis, as well as a clinical training programme in Lacanian psychoanalysis. It can provide access to Lacanian psychoanalysts working in the UK, and has links with Lacanian groups across the world. The CFAR Library aims to make classic Lacanian texts available in English for the first time, as well as publishing original research in the Lacanian field.

OTHER TITLES IN THE SERIES INCLUDE:

The Law of the Mother
An Essay on the Sexual Sinthome
by Geneviève Morel

The Baby and the Drive
Lacanian Work with Newborns and Infants
by Marie Couvert

Treating Autism Today
Lacanian Perspectives
edited by Laura Tarsia and Kristina Valendinova

www.cfar.org.uk

https://www.routledge.com/The-Centre-for-Freudian-Analysis-and-Research-Library/book-series/KARNACCFARL

Treating Autism Today

Lacanian Perspectives

Edited by
Laura Tarsia and Kristina Valendinova

LONDON AND NEW YORK

First published 2022
by Routledge
2 Park Square, Milton Park, Abingdon, Oxon OX14 4RN

and by Routledge
605 Third Avenue, New York, NY 10158

Routledge is an imprint of the Taylor & Francis Group, an informa business

© 2022 selection and editorial matter, Laura Tarsia and Kristina Valendinova; individual chapters, the contributors

The right of Laura Tarsia and Kristina Valendinova to be identified as the authors of the editorial material, and of the authors for their individual chapters, has been asserted in accordance with sections 77 and 78 of the Copyright, Designs and Patents Act 1988.

All rights reserved. No part of this book may be reprinted or reproduced or utilised in any form or by any electronic, mechanical, or other means, now known or hereafter invented, including photocopying and recording, or in any information storage or retrieval system, without permission in writing from the publishers.

Trademark notice: Product or corporate names may be trademarks or registered trademarks, and are used only for identification and explanation without intent to infringe.

British Library Cataloguing-in-Publication Data
A catalogue record for this book is available from the British Library

Library of Congress Cataloging-in-Publication Data
Names: Tarsia, Laura, editor. | Valendinova, Kristina, editor.
Title: Treating autism today : Lacanian perspectives / edited by Laura Tarsia and Kristina Valendinova.
Description: Milton Park, Abingdon, Oxon ; New York, NY : Routledge, 2022. | Series: The Centre for Freudian Analysis and Research library | Includes bibliographical references and index. |
Identifiers: LCCN 2021020148 (print) | LCCN 2021020149 (ebook) | ISBN 9781032117720 (hardback) | ISBN 9780367369897 (paperback) | ISBN 9781003221487 (ebook)
Subjects: LCSH: Autism spectrum disorders--Treatment. | Autism spectrum disorders--Treatment.
Classification: LCC RC553.A88 T733 2022 (print) | LCC RC553.A88 (ebook) | DDC 616.85/882--dc23
LC record available at https://lccn.loc.gov/2021020148
LC ebook record available at https://lccn.loc.gov/2021020149

ISBN: 978-1-032-11772-0 (hbk)
ISBN: 978-0-367-36989-7 (pbk)
ISBN: 978-1-003-22148-7 (ebk)

DOI: 10.4324/9781003221487

Typeset in Times New Roman
by Taylor & Francis Books

Contents

	List of contributors	vii
	Acknowledgements	x
	Treating autism today: Lacanian perspectives	1
1	Autism in the neoliberal age: Some reflections JACQUES HOCHMANN	13
2	The lessons of autism LEONARDO S. RODRÍGUEZ	25
3	Like the monotonous voice of the *gusle*: Some reflections on autism GRACIELA PRIETO	42
4	Autists, practitioners, and institutions: The abuse of reductionism JEAN-PIERRE DRAPIER	59
5	A psychoanalyst in the land of ABA MARIE-DOMINIQUE AMY	77
6	Psychoanalysis for autisms PATRICK LANDMAN	87
7	Diagnosing and educating autistic children today IVÁN RUIZ ACERO AND NEUS CARBONELL CAMÓS	96
8	Autism: The French debate PIERRE-HENRI CASTEL	103

9 High-functioning autism and the ideology of behaviorism 114
YANN DIENER

Afterword: What is the place of psychoanalysis in the treatment
of autism today? 119

Index 129

Contributors

Marie-Dominique Amy is a psychoanalyst, clinical psychologist, and lecturer in psychology. In 2004, she founded CIPPA, Coordination Internationale de psychologues cliniciens et de psychanalystes s'occupant de personnes autistes (International Coordination of Psychoanalytic Psychotherapists Working with Autists), of which she served as the Chair. She is the author of numerous articles and books, including *Construire et soigner la relation mère-enfant* (2008), *La relation mère-enfant* (2012), *La sécurité affective de l'enfant* (2012), *Comment aider l'enfant autiste* (2013), and *Autismes, les inquiétudes d'une psychanalyste* (2015).

Neus Carbonell Camós is a psychoanalyst in Barcelona and member of the École lacanienne de psychanalyse (Lacanian School of Psychoanalysis) (ELP) and the World Association of Psychoanalysis. She works in Early Intervention in the public healthcare system. She holds a degree in Psychology and Philology, as well as a Doctorate in Comparative Literature. She is the co-founder of TEAdir, a non-profit association for parents and relatives of people with autism.

Pierre-Henri Castel is a philosopher and historian of science at CNRS, at the Centre interdisciplinaire d'études sur les réflexivités, Fonds Yan Thomas, at the École des hautes études en sciences sociales (School of Advanced Studies in the Social Sciences) (EHESS), Paris. He also is a psychoanalyst in private practice. His recent publications include *Le Cas Paramord. Obsession et contrainte psychique aujourd'hui* (2016) and *Le Mal qui vient. Essai hâtif sur la fin des temps* (2018).

Yann Diener is a psychoanalyst in Paris and member of the ELP. A columnist at the French satirical magazine *Charlie Hebdo*, he is the author of *On agite un enfant: L'État, les psychothérapeutes et les psychotropes* (2011) and *Des histoires chiffonnées, 1938–2018* (2019).

Jean-Pierre Drapier is a psychoanalyst, analyst member of the École de psychanalyse des forums du champ lacanien (School of Psychoanalysis of the Forums of the Lacanian Field) (EPFCL), and lecturer at the Collèges de

Clinique Psychanalytique de Paris. He is the Honorary Hospital Practitioner and Clinical Director of the Medico-psychologico-pedagogical Centre (CMPP) in Orly. He has worked with autistic patients for over 30 years and continues to learn a great deal from every one of them.

Jacques Hochmann is a Professor Emeritus at the Claude-Bernard University in Lyon, Honorary Consultant at the Hospitals of Lyon, and honorary member of the Société psychanalytique de Paris. He is the founder of the Institute for the Treatment of Affectivity and Cognition Disorders (ITTAC), a diagnostic and therapeutic centre in Villeurbanne. He is the author of many books and articles, including *Histoire de l'autisme* (2009), *Pour soigner l'enfant autiste* (2010), *Une Histoire de l'Empathie* (2012), *Les Antipsychiatries, une histoire* (2015) and *Théories de la dégénérescence, d'un mythe psychiatrique au déclinisme contemporain* (2018).

Patrick Landman is a psychoanalyst and psychiatrist. He is the Chairman of the STOP DSM Initiative and the President of the Scientific Committee of the Association Autisme Espoire vers l'Ecole (AEVE), which supports parents of autistic children in the education system. He is the author of *Tous Hyperactifs?* (2015) and co-director of the report *Ce que les psychanalystes apportent à la société*, published in 2019.

Graciela Prieto is an Argentinian psychoanalyst, clinical psychologist, and researcher living and working in Paris. She is an associated researcher at the Research Centre for Psychoanalysis, Medicine and Society, Paris Diderot University and a member of the EPFCL. She is the author of *Écritures du Sinthome – Van Gogh, Schwitters, Wolman* (2013), as well as numerous articles on psychoanalysis, topology, and art.

Leonardo S. Rodríguez is a psychoanalyst. He is a founding member of the Australian Centre for Psychoanalysis and the EPFCL and former Senior Lecturer at the Department of Psychiatry, Monash University and Coordinator of the Master of Psychoanalysis programme, Victoria University. He is the author of *Psychoanalysis with Children* (1999) and numerous book chapters and articles in different languages on psychoanalytic theory and practice.

Iván Ruiz Acero is a psychoanalyst in Barcelona, member of the Escuela Lacaniana de Psicoanálisis y de la Asociación Mundial de Psicoanálisis, coordinator of the Research Group on Psychosis and Autism of the Barcelona Clinical Section of the Instituto del Campo Freudiano. He is the author, with Neus Carbonell, of *No todo sobre el autismo* (2013), and the director of the 2013 documentary *Other Voices: A different look at autism*. He is also the President of TEAdir, the association of fathers, mothers, and relatives of persons with autism.

Laura Tarsia is a psychoanalyst working with adults and young people in London. She is a member and lecturer at CFAR (Centre for Freudian Analysis and Research).

Kristina Valendinova is a psychoanalyst and translator in London, member of CFAR and of the Cercle Freudien in Paris. She is the co-founder of Bubble and Speak, a "maison verte" drop-in for small children and their carers.

Acknowledgements

The editors would like to thank all of the authors who have contributed to this collection, as well as Editions Eres, EPFCL France, and RBA Revistas, who kindly gave their permission to translate previously published texts. We also wish to thank Darian Leader and Anouchka Grose for their generous help, comments, and encouragement in preparing this volume.

The essays in this volume have been translated from French by Kristina Valendinova and from Spanish by Astrid Zeceña.

Treating autism today
Lacanian perspectives

In a democratic society, autism raises a fundamental political question of accepting or rejecting difference, one that provokes anxiety, generates a fear of the unknown, and can easily lead to segregation. In the history of psychiatry, this question is obviously not new. However, the present-day "epidemic" of autism and the subsequent backlash of "politics of neurodiversity"[1] also have to do with the changing social bond, which in the late capitalist market system increasingly fosters isolation. Perhaps this is why in common parlance we now tend to label many behaviours as "autistic", such as our obsessive use of smartphones or displaying poor social skills. It is true that any social critique, no matter how robust, always runs the risk of slipping away from the singular, i.e. the dimension most valuable to psychoanalysis. However, by listening carefully to autists and their difficulties, we can learn precious lessons about human functioning more generally.

In today's culture, this attention to the singular is not always on the agenda. The DSM has managed to erase from the mental health map those nosological categories that favoured a conception of human subjectivity based on listening to individual stories of suffering and today's psychiatry has moved towards a strictly biological orientation, relying on the detection of symptoms for which the pharmaceutical industry can offer the appropriate drug. In this context, by doing a quick search on Google, we learn that autism is a developmental disorder characterised by difficulties with social interaction and communication, and by restricted and repetitive behaviour. It is usually diagnosed once a child is perceived to experience social delays, communication problems, and behavioural symptoms. Since both social and communication challenges are part of the autism diagnosis, behavioural and speech therapies typically comprise the basis of a treatment plan. Most of these methods, which emerged in the United States and subsequently spread to Europe, are of the cognitive-behavioural ilk and function as protocols applied to re-educate the child. As a popular ADHD-focused online magazine puts it:

> With autism, the foundation of intervention is behavioral therapy. Behavioral programs do not only address disruptive behaviors. Interventions

DOI: 10.4324/9781003221487-1

such as applied behavioral analysis (ABA) therapy are the primary tools for teaching social skills. ...

One predictor of a good outcome is the application of ongoing behavioral therapy, regardless of severity of symptoms. Think of it this way: If you want your child to be a concert pianist or a professional athlete, he or she should practice a lot each day. The same goes for social skills.

(Bertin, 2018)

Since it is the *social appearance* of the autistic subject that is being treated by behavioural therapy, we may legitimately wonder about the effects of its zealous application, both intended and unintended. Is it really beneficial to suppress overt symptoms such as repetitions or stereotypies? Should behavioural adjustment be the primary goal of therapy? How do autistic children learn? Would reinforcement of ongoing behavioural and social skills allow a child to have more natural and less threatening social interactions? And if there is little or no social interaction initially, what lies behind this absence and what can be done about it, aside from a reprogramming of surface behaviour? Since autism is so often diagnosed via box-ticking a list of pre-set categories and developmental markers, the human being is effectively reduced to his or her behaviour. In the age of "surveillance capitalism" which commodifies consumer behaviour by leveraging data-processing technologies on an unprecedented scale (Zuboff, 2019), this predilection for interventions targeting the observable and quantifiable parts of human experience – while disregarding the question of their meaning entirely – should not surprise us.[2] And yet, as Lacanian psychoanalysts Neus Carbonell and Iván Ruiz (Carbonell & Ruiz, 2013) explain, when the autistic subject is forced to fit certain social ideals – saying what is appropriate in each interaction, smiling only at appropriate moments, abandoning interests considered "strange" by others, etc. – what is achieved is simply the annihilation of the subjective dimension. The rigid and mechanical language these treatments sometimes encourage in effect produce a kind of subjective silence. In this sense, "treating" autism inadvertently just creates ... a different kind of autism.

In contrast to this model, many psychoanalysts have tried to find more singular solutions for the autistic subject, solutions that do not rely on social norms. In July 2007, in order to address the lack of dialogue among different traditions of research into autism, CFAR held a conference on autism,[3] bringing the continental psychoanalytic perspectives on autism to a British audience. Our book wishes to take a similar path and open up new perspectives in thinking about autism.

The biological hypothesis

The clinical prevalence of autism has risen astonishingly in recent decades: during the 1990s, the UK saw a fivefold increase in the annual incidence rates, while the Centers for Disease Control and Prevention cited a 78% increase in the Unites States between 2004 and 2008 (Taylor et al., 2013). However, the current trend towards assessment and evaluation means that empirically available phenomena are quantified – via tests, protocols, measurement of stereotypies – without questioning the complexity of what is supposedly being measured. The diagnosis of autism thus risks becoming a generalisation that merely approximates the problems each child experiences, leaving out the specificity and singularity of each case. Whereas early research paid great attention to this singular dimension, what was once a rigorous approach to the causes and implications of autism has now been lost. While autism sparks enormous interest in the media, with grand claims often making headlines, little is actually known about it, and caring for autistic subjects is a highly specialised field. The new therapeutic guidelines are reductionist in terms of the complexity of the problem and tell us little about the life-long care needed by autistic subjects or the directions their life may take.

In its issue devoted to "the autism enigma", the prestigious scientific journal Nature (2011) agrees that despite an enormous amount of research funding, a rigorous scientific knowledge of the causes of autism continues to elude us.

Until today, it has proven impossible to establish a simple causal relationship between genetics and the phenomena observed in autistic subjects. The current scenario in which everything is explained biologically cannot be understood without factoring in the force exerted by the market on scientific research and policymaking, in the form of health bureaucracies allied with the pharmaceutical industry. Autism today is big business and this fact alone favours the coalescence of new treatments with drugs, and with a broadly biological understanding.

Yet, without trying to exclude biological and genetic factors, the question is still how a given subject responds to them. Scientism promotes normative standards and subjects who deviate from them are left open to stigma, rather than being considered in their difference. And even when the diagnosis is presented as not carrying any kind of judgement and, in some contexts, providing valuable forms of recognition, this leaves out the anxiety that an autistic subject may feel when subjected to re-education methods. Autists are often grouped together according to similarities rather than differences, and treated as if they were a passive object upon which re-education is applied. There is no margin here for the active and unpredictable position of the subject, and little room for helping them articulate and develop their own individual solutions.

A diagnosis of autism involves having a hypothesis about both diagnostic and prognostic questions, and therefore a proposal for treatment. If the hypothesis is of a neurophysiological disorder that leads the autistic subject to exhibit "bad" social behaviours, this tends to entail that all the behaviours that a child enacts outside the standard social norms will be understood negatively, and he will be encouraged to substitute them with "good" ones. Typical re-education methods have as one of their main objectives the avoidance of "problematic behaviours", so that the child learns (sometimes at quite a cost) the most socially appropriate responses. But do the behaviours that these methods aim to excise have a function for the child? Do the questions parents raise with professionals about their child – rather than the child's brain – have a meaning?

The psychoanalytic hypothesis

In all this debate, the assumption of a psychic causality is excluded. There is virtually no place for human subjectivity, that is to say, for the way in which a given subject deals with the particular experiences of his life. For Lacanian psychoanalysis, the origins of autism, as in the case of any psychic structure, cannot be located in any distinct area of the brain and do not follow any simple cause-and-effect model. Instead, psychoanalysis looks towards language as the only "cause" that we can access; and between this cause and its effects, there is the subject, in the case of autism a subject in a rather precarious position – on the edge of the world, just before being caught entirely by it.

Lacanian psychoanalysis indeed starts from the hypothesis that *there is a subject in autism*, one who has adopted a radical position vis-à-vis the world as a protection against anxiety. In this perspective, their behaviours – including behaviours impeded by neurophysiological deficiencies or delays – can be seen as meaningful, as properly human. There is always a subjective dimension to be found and the way a subject is positioned in relation to their world – which includes their neurological structure, genetics, and the environment in which they live – is what psychoanalysis focuses on, what it wishes to restore to the autistic person and in this way give dignity to their unique world. According to Alexandre Stevens, the former director of *Le Courtil*, one of the psychoanalytically informed institutions for psychotic and autistic children in Belgium, what matters is understanding what the logic at stake is for each child and using it to help him or her construct a subjective position. Carbonell and Ruiz write:

> Autism is recognizable by the withdrawal into himself that the child effects at a very early stage of development, in which the child protects himself from a world that he perceives as tremendously hostile. At that moment, the autistic subject's position was to say a radical NO to everything that involved a dependence on the Other (symbolic, order of language, social other) in order to enter the world. ... This is what many parents can detect as the moment when their child stopped looking at them or smiling, refused to accept any kind of change, even small changes of food or habits, and when the few words he had started to be able to say, suddenly disappeared.

The autistic "bubble" is established as an extreme mode of protection, to the point of not differentiating between the subject and his defences. The child's efforts are directed at building a world at his own pace and under his control; his satisfaction is confined to his own body or obtained by means of various objects.

Michel Silvestre (1997, p. 9) argues that autism is a fundamental manifestation of the human being's relation to speech, drawing on the distinction between the function of speech and language as a field established by Lacan in *Function and Field of Speech and Language*. The autistic person has problems with the function of speech – but because he has parents, a family, neighbours, etc., he or she is living, like the rest of us, in the field of language. Therefore, we have a particular difficulty with these children, because although, like everyone else, they are taken up in the field of language, because of the shortcomings of the function of the speech, we are left without access to them as subjects. We have to ask ourselves how we can introduce them to the function of speech. They are in language but have not appropriated its codes. This leaves them outside discourse, and for many, outside all social ties. They thus avoid any position of enunciation.

One of the key issues in the treatment of autism lies here. Re-education methods may teach the autistic subject to speak certain words at certain times, but is this really the same thing as taking up a position of enunciation? And if this were at all possible, what would its conditions be? For some analysts, there must be a change in the relation of the autistic subject to their body. Psychoanalyst Sergio Laia (2015, p. 105) in his article comparing the spectral dimension of autism in the DSM-V and the Lacanian dimension of jouissance, reminds us that already Eugen Bleuler (1911, p. 112) had linked autism to autoerotism. It may be the case that in the bodies of autistic subjects there is an "excitation" that manifests not only at the moments when they are disturbed in their loneliness. This "sum of excitation" evoked by Freud, regarding the impact of affects on the body and anticipating the vicissitudes he later identifies in the satisfaction of the drives (1915), is a non-quantifiable dimension distinct from the biological parameters but nonetheless closely linked to the body, the substance Lacan called "jouissance". Lacanian work has elucidated this bodily dimension and shown how a Lacanian approach can not only help us conceptualise it but also offers clinical indications for treatment.

Lacanian psychoanalytic approaches to treatment and to learning

Among the first Lacanian psychoanalysts working with autistic subjects, Rosine and Robert Lefort report on two cases in their pivotal 1980 book *Birth of the Other*. Rosine Lefort's treatment, in the early 1950s, of two children in care, 13-month-old Nadia and 30-month-old Marie-Françoise, are described here in detail. Both turn around the radical, real absence of the Other for the two abandoned children, despite the fact that the two treatments have very different outcomes. In this work, the child is treated as a subject in her own right. The analyst's approach may at times seem strikingly passive: Lefort lets herself be hit, slapped, bitten, etc., yet she remains highly attentive to the work carried out by the child in her presence and maintaining the analytical position of responding to the child without trying to satisfy a need.

In a later work, *La Distinction de l'Autisme*, which looks at the lives of a number of what would be today considered "high-functioning" autists, the Leforts explain that the inherent genius of autism lies in the autist's "response to the Real, where he finds his mask: to create an empty space" (2003, p. 183). The radical absence of the Other pushes the subject towards creation: "Faced with the horror speech that manifests as real, the creationist, divine perspective of the work of art, of religion or science can become the privileged field of autism" (ibid.).

The Experimental School in Bonneuil-sur-Marne, founded by the psychoanalyst Maud Mannoni in 1969 as a live-in community caring for children with autism and severe psychosis and reformed as a day hospital in 1975, was inspired by both psychoanalysis and the anti-psychiatry movement of that time. From Winnicott, who had once been her supervisor, Mannoni adopted her understanding of these conditions as not simply pathological processes, but reactions against extremely conflictual life situations. She wanted the School to be a different place, where adults and children together took care of their living space. Though some children follow a curriculum, the School's mission is not primarily pedagogical; rather than a simple accumulation of knowledge, it promotes a relationship to learning where culture is present, yet educational ideology is constantly questioned. The adult staff do not refer to expert knowledge, which, as Mannoni believed, would only serve their own defences toward the child's subjective conflicts and difficulties and obscure the effect of truth inherent in the child's "symptomatic discourse" (Vanier & Malone, 2017). Through the different daily activities (cooking, shopping), art practices, and discussions, the staff tries to offer the children

> the possibility of doing something *with* their symptom, in order to make their life more bearable, and help them discover that they are not simply the sick children so often marginalized and objects of treatment, but also subjects who can take the risk of confronting their desire.

Mannoni described Bonneuil as an "inside-outside institution" (*institution éclatée*), stressing the openness and porousness of the framework, which, while constituting a solid ground, also allows for gaps and openings towards its surroundings, and thus for inventiveness and the unexpected – a form of resistance against the increasing rationalisation and bureaucratisation of both the educational and the mental health systems. This is why, Catherine Vanier writes, since its creation, Bonneuil has remained a thorn in the side of the authorities:

We do not ask the child to adapt to society, but society to adapt to the child, so that he can gradually tame the anxiety that cuts him off from the rest of the world and find a place that is his own.

(ibid.)

Two Belgian institutions, Antenne 110 and Le Courtil, founded, respectively, in the 1970s and 1980s, similarly straddle the line between therapeutic work and education. The "educators" work within a psychoanalytic frame of reference, offering the child a "partnership" in order to treat what is unbearable for him or her. They follow the child's individual needs to help construct objects and circuits that make their world more liveable. The former director of Antenne 110, Virginio Baio explains that the Latin word *educere* is derived from *ex* and *ducere*, which means "to drive, to bring out", i.e. *to educate* designates the operation of "driving out", and hence, in the case of an autistic child, may consist of extracting the subject from the position of an object of jouissance, towards helping them become a creature of language. Baio explains that these children are always "at work" when they come to see us – in play, in how they manage their objects (Baio, 2002, p. 2). Beneath the stereotypies and repetitive gestures there is a subject trying to inscribe, to anchor, to articulate a construction.

The question of what place should be given, in the treatment, to stereotypies, echolalia, and similar phenomena, is thus one of the key points of divergence between behavioural methods, which most often strive to eliminate or suppress them, and psychoanalytic therapies. The latter consider these behaviours as subjective productions to be respected and as valuable indices of what might be at stake for that particular child, as well as teaching us something about the logic of autism more generally. The neurolinguist Theo Peeters, an advocate of the TEACCH method, agrees that "certain rituals and repetitive behaviour of autistic people are avoidance mechanisms" (1997, p. 148), in other words, they are not devoid of sense and have a function for the subject. Peeters argues that instead of waiting (in vain) for the autistic person to adapt to a challenging environment, the environment must first adapt to his or her abilities; it must be given meaning and clarity.[4]

Among the key criteria of the ever-expanding diagnosis of autism is a lack of relationship between the autistic child and others and their difficulties in verbal communication. Yet psychoanalytic and other case studies have demonstrated that the relationship with others is not necessarily always absent; it may manifest as a "subtle bond", which the clinician must be taught by the autistic child to recognise and understand. The psychoanalytic approach is relational, based on the signs of interest shown by the child. It is a bespoke solicitation. Autistic children protect themselves from the word. They maintain a highly complex relation with both the signifier and the object-voice. As the authors in this book describe, children may feel threatened, persecuted by the signifier, as well as the object-voice. Hence treatments which focus on demand, on the application of a predetermined plan, may be antithetical to the basic structure of autism.

As Tendlarz observes,

> Upon receiving an autistic child, the analyst seeks to make contact with him without being experienced as invasive. By trying to be by the child's side, to get to know his passions, his world, what his interests are and what resources he has. We should not force him to give up some of these behaviours and interests in the name of what he would normally have to do, nor teach him how to behave.
>
> (Tendlarz, 2015, p. 127)

The analyst must be careful not to be perceived as intrusive or persecutory, as a threat to the child's closed universe. The only way of intervening lies in carefully accompanying the child in his singular trajectory, helping to make his life more liveable.

In Lacanian work, the focus is thus placed on helping the autistic subject to invent some form of support, a singular invention which can create some kind of link with the Other. The analyst will have to make him or herself available for this unique work – being taught by the autistic subject rather than trying to teach him something. The position of the subject is the compass that orients, in effect, any analytic action. This does not mean to simply leave the child to his stereotypies, repetitions, etc., but while respecting these phenomena as the child's first line of defence, the analyst may then discreetly try to introduce new elements, opening up new possibilities for the subject.

Perspectives in this volume

In addition to presenting some aspects of Lacanian work with autism in more detail, the texts in this collection also analyse the conceptual and ideological underpinnings of the mainstream models of autism and the behavioural and cognitive approaches popular today. We include works by a range of leading clinicians who follow a Lacanian perspective in their research and clinical work with autistic children and share their often divergent and novel perspectives on diagnosis, aetiology, and treatment.

In the first chapter, Jacques Hochmann situates the history of autism in France within the larger history of post-World War II psychiatry, its links to political and economic institutions, and the establishment of the welfare state. In his view, the recent extension of the "autistic spectrum" could be connected to the ideology of neoliberalism, which "packages" certain identities as products, selling "a growing number of copies to state authorities expected to treat it and to private funders asked to charitably support it". The logic of cost-cutting, the dictatorship of public opinion, and the emphasis on "compassion" as an immediate inter-individual identification with the victim, which replaces the social bond of the past, all combine to further the transactional ideal of the individual as a constantly self-optimising micro-enterprise.

In his essay, Leonardo Rodríguez sees autism as "a failure in the establishment of *lalangue,* the material basis of language and of the first modality of human discourse". The autist, like the psychotic, is not in discourse. His text stresses the principle of singularity which orients psychoanalytic work as a clinical and ethical principle. Rodríguez explains how "typical" parameters of the psychoanalytic experience of discourse should not operate as constraints; the analyst's creativity and inventiveness, his willingness to listen without demanding anything are needed here perhaps more than ever. Autism "is not radically curable; yet clinical experience shows that … for autistic patients and their families the analytic treatment makes quite a difference".

Graciela Prieto explores the ways in which the present-day model of a purely bio-genetic causality of autism contorts actual scientific discoveries. Prieto emphasises that the current neuroscientific theories draw on technologies that are depicted as providing accurate readings of brain activity, yet in fact rely on interpretations of highly complex data processed on the basis of our still imperfect knowledge, often mistaking correlation for causation. The research on brain plasticity has in fact made the difficulty of attributing behavioural phenomena to specific areas of the brain even more obvious. Her understanding of autistic symptoms relies on Lacan theorisation of the "solidification" of the signifying chain. The autistic symptom does not constitute a separate structure, but rather a specific modality of "making do" with foreclosure.

Jean-Pierre Drapier calls for a more rigorous diagnosis of autism. The current diagnostic label of autism attempts to bring together, under the same category, cases of highly heterogeneous aetiology and development, meaning that the formal envelope of the symptom can easily obscure structural differences requiring very different therapeutic strategies. Drapier instead prefers to speak about the "autistic syndrome", which he defines based on three characteristics: the sense of persecution by the signs of the Other's existence, a defence that tries to abolish this Other, and the absence of a structured body image. This syndrome is a trans-structural construction that covers or conceals an underlying structure – a psychosis or neurosis – every time there is an impediment in the subject's access to signifying alienation.

How can psychoanalysis and an education approach such as ABA work together? Marie-Dominique Amy in the fifth chapter shares her experience of working with autistic children in settings which tended to favour the psychodynamic approach to the exclusion of others. She argues that the divisions and disputes between the different orientations and professionals in fact only harm autistic patients, whose existing splits they further reinforce, rather than helping them make new links between their experience and feelings. While psychoanalysts criticise educational approaches as a form of "robotisation", they are often rigid in their view of the cure as a process of "emergence of desire" and resistant to the role personalised cognitive learning can play in helping children and adolescents manage difficult emotions. According to her, both extremes demonstrate a deep misunderstanding of the fundamental issue in autism, namely the failure of consubstantiality. Amy's plea is for a "double reading": an approach to autism that focuses both on cognition and emotional experience: treating only one or the other is counterproductive.

Patrick Landman examines the reasons why psychoanalysis has been marginalised as a treatment approach to autism and argues that it remains relevant under certain conditions and especially as part of a pluralistic and interdisciplinary approach to autism. The fact that in the DSM autism is diagnosed exclusively based on observable behaviour means that the therapeutic method also tends to be exclusively behaviourist. The research that documents the efficacy of psychoanalysis in the treatment of autism tends to be disregarded, because it does not fit the evidence-based framework of established treatment protocols. Contrary to the definition of autism as a neuro-developmental disorder, psychoanalysis offers the idea of a "failure of access to intersubjectivity", a dynamic process which can potentially benefit from a psychoanalytic intervention, particularly at an early stage.

Iván Ruiz Acero and Neus Carbonell Camós present a case vignette, in which the suspension of diagnosis was a necessary condition for the treatment of a child with autistic symptoms. Diagnosing autism requires a hypothesis about its aetiology and also a proposition of treatment. If this hypothesis is that of a neurophysiological disorder, the only possible strategy seems to be to eradicate the "unsuitable" behaviours, often at the cost of subjecting the person to highly intrusive techniques. However, if we suppose that there is a subject in the autistic child who has taken a radical stance towards the surrounding world as a necessary measure against anxiety, these behaviours can be given meaning and worked with to help the individual construct other means of negotiating the relationship with the other.

Pierre-Henri Castel shows that the recent French debate between those who oppose the use of psychoanalysis in the treatment of autism and those who defend the "clinic of the subject" reflects a larger value conflict centred on the issue of autonomy. According to Castel, the two camps share a certain blindness to their own socio-historical determinants, instead claiming a kind of transcendence, which "feeds monsters of abstraction". In order to introduce some distanciation to these questions and show the social rather than epistemological nature of the dispute, he examines a recent sociological study of an autistic treatment centre in France. Through a careful analysis of the material, he shows how biological approaches are valorised at the expense of human relations involved in families, to create a picture of autism as a uniquely biological problem. The therapies that are then indicated serve as vehicles for hidden psychological processes involving guilt, blame, and displacement.

In the final essay of this volume, Yann Diener asks the timely question of the possible effects of the growing digitisation of our world on us, speaking beings. It did not take computers to complicate human relationships, he writes, but the current prioritising of the language *code*, the loss of differentiation between speaking and writing due to the use of instant messaging and our growing discomfort with direct speech leave less space for speaking, for the singular, for desire and surprise. The ideological underpinnings of the concept of "high-functioning autism", which valorises these traits, implicitly separating these individuals from "low-functioning" autists, have recently been revealed in a historian's account of the Vienna psychiatrist Hans Asperger, one of the first to describe autism, whose active involvement in the Nazi eugenics programme has now become abundantly clear.

We wish to express our thanks to the authors of these essays.

Notes

1 The term "neurodiversity" was first promoted by the sociologist Judy Singer, who self-identifies as Asperger's, in her 1999 article, "Why can't you be normal for once in your life?" Its proponents criticise the framing of autism and other supposed neurodevelopmental disorders as pathologies requiring a cure and call for more acknowledgement of autistic capabilities, as well as support for different forms of human diversity and self-expression.
2 These interventions now include a plethora of educational and other apps, a fascinating area of overlap between what is marketed as therapeutic and educational support and the "quantified self". In addition to apps that aid communication by using multisensory interfaces, these are often aimed at helping children learn "positive social behaviour", for instance by modelling appropriate and expected interactions in typified settings (a hairdresser's, a doctor's office, a restaurant), or help parents track their child's daily behaviours "so you can discover what's working and what needs to be changed".
3 The theoretical issues addressed by the *Children's Minds: New Perspectives on Autism* conference included: if autism is often associated with language difficulties, what theory of language do we need to make sense of it? If the autistic child has problems in relating to others, what notion of "other" would help us to understand these problems? What sort of conception of the body do we need to explain the unusual relation to surfaces in autism? And what can a therapy with an autistic child achieve?
4 More so than others, the TEACCH method emphasises individualised one-to-one programmes; however, these are conducted in a highly secured and structured environment, outside of which they have generally have poor outcomes. "Effects over adaptive behavioural repertoires including communication, activities of daily living, and motor functioning were within the negligible to small range" (Virués-Ortega et al., 2013). This particularity of the intervention setting is equally an issue for other approaches, such as *Floortime* or *3i*, which also turn away from a rigid blanket approach and towards a more individualised, low-intrusion, and play-based learning.

References

Baio, V. (2002). Cito tute iucunde: a clinic with an autistic subject. *Courtil Papers*, 9.
Bertin, M. (2018). Autism and ADHD: the complete playbook for social challenges. *Attitude Magazine*. Retrieved on 1 July 2020 from www.additudemag.com/autism-and-adhd.
Bleuler, E. (1911 [1993]). *Dementia praecox ou groupe des schizophrenies*. Paris: EPEL.

Carbonell, N. & Ruiz, I. (2013). *No todo sobre el autismo*. Barcelona: Editorial Gredos.

Freud, S. (1915). Instincts and their vicissitudes. *Standard Edition* (Vol. 14, p. 109–140). London: Hogarth Press.

Laia, S. (2015). El autismo: Su dimension Espectral en el DSM-5 y la dimension lacaniana del GOCE. In Tendlarz, S.E. (Ed.), *Estudios sobre el Autismo II*. Buenos Aires: Collection Diva, pp. 101–116.

Laurent, E. (2012). *La Bataille de l'autisme*. Paris: Navarin.

Lefort, R. & Lefort, R. (1980). *Birth of the Other*. Translated by M. du Ry, L. Watson and L. Rodríguez. Urbana, IL: University of Chicago.

Lefort, R. & Lefort, R. (2003). *La distinction de l'autisme*. Paris: Seuil.

Nature (2011). Special issue on neuroscience: the autism enigma. *Nature*, 479(7371), 21.

Peeters, T. (1997). *Autism: From Theoretical Understanding to Educational Intervention*. Hoboken, NJ: Wiley-Blackwell.

Sylvestre, M. (1997). L'autisme infantile. *L'Autisme, Bulletin du Groupe Petite Enfance*, 10, 9.

Taylor, B., Jick, H., MacLaughlin, D. (2013). Prevalence and incidence rates of autism in the UK: time trend from 2004–2010 in children aged 8 years. *BMJOpen*, 3, 1–6.

Tendlarz, S.E. (Ed.) (2015). *Estudios sobre el autismo II*. Buenos Aires: Coleccion Diva.

Vanier, C. & Malone, K. (2017). The Experimental School in Bonneuil-sur-Marne… with commentary from a North American context. *Frontiers in Psychology*, 8(1794).

Virués-Ortega, J., Julio, F. & Pastor-Barriuso, R. (2013). The TEACCH program for children and adults with autism: a meta-analysis of intervention studies. *Clinical Psychology Review*, 33, 940–953.

Zuboff, S. (2019). *The Age of Surveillance Capitalism*. London: Profile Books.

Chapter 1

Autism in the neoliberal age
Some reflections[1]

Jacques Hochmann

Since its very beginnings, the history of psychiatry in France has been linked to certain political and economic institutions. Inspired by the ideas of the Enlightenment and their expression in the French Revolution, it saw its first large-scale deployment in alienist medicine and its historical birthplace, the asylum, and subsequently experienced a regression during the Second Empire (1852–1870) and the Third Republic (1870–1940). The overcrowded asylums lost all of their therapeutic potential and instead became places of exclusion dominated by the practices of restraint. Meanwhile, leading theories attributed mental disorder to either a degeneracy of the human species or a hereditary pathological constitution, in other words, a genetic defect quasi-impossible to correct, which could only be prevented from propagating itself through segregation or eugenics. Research focused on finding a supposedly obvious organic cause by carrying out, only exceptionally with any results, a growing number of autopsies and histological brain studies. ECT and psychosurgery brought a new confidence, a hope for more active types of therapy, but in fact led to ethically inadmissible excesses. While the Popular Front seemed to have a brief moment of realisation about the true scale of neglect affecting the incarcerated mentally ill population, it was only during the rich period of Liberation, when a new social security system was created, that French psychiatry, emerging from the massacres of psychiatric inmates during World War II, experienced a genuine rebirth. We owe a debt to a whole generation of militant psychiatrists, often former members of the Resistance, for the subsequent enactment of the French sector policy and the unprecedented diversification of the responses to mental pathology: more human hospital conditions, less marginalising community treatment, approaching the patient as a subject and, especially, a greater efficiency due to the joint development of chemotherapies and psychotherapies, mostly inspired by psychoanalysis. This larger movement, which in the UK contributed to the creation of the National Health Service and the Community Psychiatry movement, in the United States to the 1963 Kennedy Mental Health Act, in Italy to the Basaglia Law, voted in with the support of the Italian Left, also inspired similar types of activism in the English-speaking parts of Canada and Quebec, in

DOI: 10.4324/9781003221487-2

Switzerland, Belgium, Holland, and Germany. After these brilliant beginnings, which in Argentina were impeded by the tyranny of the dictatorship, the movement gradually spread further, to Spain, Greece, Portugal, and throughout the democratic world.

The history of autism is only a particularly interesting example of this development, interrupted by periods of regression. Child autism was first diagnosed, virtually at the same time, by two authors separated by the war: the American child psychiatrist Leo Kanner and the Austrian paediatrician Hans Asperger. It was initially studied by psychodynamic psychiatrists – neither Kanner nor Asperger had any psychoanalytic references, but they both belonged to currents that contributed to the birth of psychopathology.[2] Both clinicians described a process in which symptoms were not just the expression of a cerebral lesion or a passively experienced dysfunction, but were part of a complex picture, functioning as adaptations or defence mechanisms. In his princeps description, Kanner repeatedly uses active verbs to describe the action through which an autistic child distances himself from the other, excludes or ignores everything that disrupts his need for unchangeability. Likewise, Asperger emphasises the ingenuity of the young "autistic psychopath", his "will" to manipulate the other as a material object in order to control the other's uncanny strangeness. While Kanner followed a category-based approach and remained convinced that he was delineating the field of a true illness, akin to phenylketonuria and clearly separated from the state of normalcy and from other associated illnesses like schizophrenia, Asperger's approach was more dimensional, close to Kurt Schneider's description of "pathological personalities", the limits of which bordered on normality.[3] However, both broke away from reducing the child's problems to simply a cognitive deficit, measured on a metric scale. They showed that such method was unsuitable to studying this type of multidimensional developmental disharmony and instead tried to approach the child's mental pathology more optimistically. Seeing it as an individualised and highly specific "innate disorder of affective contact", which did not necessarily involve an intellectual deficit, Kanner wished to save at least some of the supposedly mentally disabled children from the practices of sterilisation and castration still popular not so long ago. (We remember the castration of Benjy, the hero of *The Sound and the Fury*, a typical autist described by Faulkner 15 years before Kanner's publication.)

Although some organicist neuropsychiatrists continued, still without any major successes, to use their EEG and pneumoencephalographies, and later more modern imaging techniques to try to detect brain lesions, it was mostly thanks to the psychoanalytically oriented psychiatrists and psychologists that the nosography of autism was refined, treatments promoted, and psychopathological hypotheses elaborated to connect practice with theory. The minority rights and civil rights struggles, as well as the anti-war protests in the United States, the struggle against the colonial wars in France, the critique of capitalism by the far-left in Germany or Italy, the Antipsychiatry movement in the UK – i.e. all that helped prepare, in various forms, the explosion of 1968 – laid the grounds for these hypotheses to be received.

Already at the end of World War II, the American psychoanalyst Margaret Mahler put in place joint mother-child psychotherapies and coined the term "infantile psychosis", which she considered less confusing than "infantile schizophrenia", i.e. a diagnosis imported from adult psychiatry. She considered it was impossible to use the same term to denote the lack of integration in a developing individual and the dissociation in a mature psyche. She also suggested a distinction, within the group of infantile psychoses and following a psychopathological perspective, which included her own version of child developmental stages, between *autistic psychoses* and the so-called *symbiotic psychoses*.

In the UK, Melanie Klein's successors, especially Frances Tustin and Donald Meltzer, differentiated, respectively, between *encapsulated secondary autism* and *regressive secondary autism*, and *autism with adhesive identification* and *psychosis with excessive projective identification*. Based on her experience with lengthy and intensive treatments, Tustin formulated her theory of the "black hole", a moment of rupture that produces a psychic tearing, experienced by the child at weaning. Meltzer considered the autistic symptoms to be constructions meant to repair the breakdown suffered by the child in the moments of autistic disorganisation.

In France, it was primarily the work of Roger Misès, who suggested a tripartite distinction between autism, psychotic disharmony, and deficit psychoses, with the diagnoses of infantile schizophrenia and dysthymic psychosis being reserved for the rarest cases evolving into adult psychoses. These diagnostic indications were based on years of observation and the detection of specific anxieties and psychopathological mechanisms: the autistic auto-sensuality, the denial of reality, projection, or psychotic splitting, without confining the child to a fixed diagnosis. Instead, there was space for development, which could be encouraged by implementing dynamic and individualised programmes combing care, education, and pedagogy, in institutions that have been reformed through revolutionary ideas – these too keeping with the zeitgeist. It was shaped by governments and officials who, though not necessarily left-leaning, were nevertheless imbued by the post-World War II social-democratic ethos and the idea of the welfare state as the guardian of the social contract and protector of public services.

It was the psychoanalytically oriented psychiatrists who – as we tend to forget – brought specialised educators, teachers, speech and movement therapists, and psychologists into institutions previously devoted solely to guardianship. It was they who tried to make these places more open to the outside world and create semi-residential facilities and part-time reception and consultation centres. Having convinced the very reticent National Education, they were able to open a number – regrettably small yet preceding the present-day legislation by many years – of specialised classes to integrate severely disabled children in ordinary schools. A collaboration emerged between two traditionally separate fields: the recently organised health care sector of child and adolescent psychiatry and the pre-existing medico-social field devoted to caring for "maladjusted children" (*enfance inadaptée*). Different networks were constituted, bringing together, in separate yet coordinated spaces, academic, educational, and therapeutic processes and offering solutions adapted to different types of children at different stages of development.

In the medico-social sector, the successors of the old child protection charities joined up with family associations already after World War II. In the 1970s, a myriad of small non-profits working in social innovation also emerged, supported by public authorities. These institutions, which became known as "intermediaries", were in a sense a mixture of the best and the worst aspects of institutional care. Frequently headed by a charismatic leader, some of them explored original ways of supporting autistic and psychotic children in a kind of "communal living", often in the countryside and drawing on agricultural and artisanal activities as therapeutic mediations. Most of them tried to experiment with new models of self-governance, arguing that it was difficult to expect staff to be involved in their work personally and creatively if they had no say over its organisation. Here again, context mattered. In the aftermath of May 1968, previous forms of hierarchy and authority were put in question and the emphasis was on exchange and dialogue as microsocial processes leading to self-discovery in a relationship with others.

Unfortunately, some of these intermediary institutions, which did not sufficiently elaborate the counter-tendencies triggered by communal living and contaminated by the emotional chaos that can affect anyone cohabiting with psychosis, sometimes descended into a glorified and vaguely anarchist refusal of all rules or laws, while waiting, with a certain fascination, for the child's desire to emerge. Combined with the proliferation of an anti-family ideology very much in fashion at the time, which attributed, without a shadow of a proof, the child's psychosis to the unconscious positions of the parents – particularly the mother – and promoted a separation from the family, these excesses were often taken to express the psychoanalytic view of autism in general. In fact, they were only very distantly related to psychoanalysis. Those psychoanalysts who were most serious about caring for autistic and psychotic patients never succumbed to this type of psychogenetic simplification. They never refused to consider the hypothetical neurobiological and genetic factors (mostly unknown or only applicable to a very small number of cases), which in no way contradicted the identification of psychopathological mechanisms at a different level of analysis. They always argued that the indications of classical psychoanalytic treatments in cases of autism or psychoses were limited; mostly these were psychoanalytically inspired psychotherapies, which nevertheless made room for the specificities of the psychotic or autistic pathology. They contended that when psychotherapies were used, they could not be separated from a broader treatment programme including educational and pedagogical methods; that the function of psychoanalysis was most often to support the caregivers in their work, helping them elaborate the confused emotions transmitted to them by the children and provide a theory and models of mental functioning to inform and give meaning to the events in the institution's day-to-day life. They always emphasised the need for a close collaboration with the parents. Their calls for greater rigour were not always heard; hence the caricature of psychoanalysis popularised by the media and clumsily taken up by a number of more or less well-trained professionals. This provoked a violent reaction from some of the family support groups, at first in the United States, who called for a return to narrowly neurodevelopmental conceptions excluding any reference to environmental factors. Such approaches made autism again based on genetics alone and successfully fought for the term "infantile psychosis" to be dropped (first from the DSM and later from international classifications) as supposedly carrying negative connotations by referring exclusively to parental responsibility and, more implicitly, to madness. It is curious that in France, where this struggle was later taken up as well, it was those who were most involved in defending the dignity of autists and stood up most strongly against objectivising and dehumanising attitudes who were accused of abuse and threatened with legal action. Their thoughts and practices have been condemned, likely by misinformed ethics committees, while the authorities, having forgotten their previous positions and turning towards a new kind of policies, did nothing to defend their own employees against defamation.

The new autism policy

Today, under the growing influence of parent support groups, who are increasingly gaining a voice in society, we are seeing the gradual extension of the "autistic spectrum". Autism, which was initially included in the "pervasive developmental disorders" category that replaced the category of psychoses, has now become the core of these disorders, while others are defined more or less in relation to it. These other PDDs now only have a purely negative definition and no diagnostic scale of their own; as a result, the category of "PDD – further unspecified" has been growing as well. This is combined with, on the one hand, the designation of the autistic syndrome which can encompass a large number of severe mental disabilities and, on the other hand, the poorly defined Asperger's syndrome, which covers a large population of individuals of normal intelligence but with cognitive and emotional specificities that can inhibit their academic and social adaptation. We have thus moved from the still-recent prevalence of 0.05% to 1% and, according to a recent British study, 3% of the general population. This exponential increase in the prevalence of autism is announced, regularly and quasi-triumphantly, by the Autism Society of America, akin to a company publishing its annual accounts.[4] Autism thus seems to be a kind of product, sold in a growing number of copies to the state authorities expected to treat it and to private funders asked to charitably support it. The company's competitiveness and performance are judged by its results: the more diagnosed autists, the more the company thrives. Its marketing incites users to demand this diagnosis and professionals to deliver it, while constantly broadening its criteria of inclusion.

In France, the knowledge base on autism that the government is preparing to publish, as an obligatory framework for clinicians and their educators, only serves to formalise the perspective of certain families (whose voice resounds most loudly and denounces public psychiatry most powerfully). Following the American model, we have already been issued the diagnostic "good practice" and will see a single perspective promoted as the sole authority on the nature of autism (which nevertheless remains full of mystery) and its treatment. To temper this kind of worrisome enthusiasm, we nevertheless have to ask: is it really the task of the state, or at least the democratic state as we have known it until now, to issue scientific laws? Does the confusion between the law of the community, majority public opinion and scientific laws, which are established and constantly tested by a limited community of experts, besides doing little to actually advance science, normally opposed to the types of appreciable evidence that sway public opinion, also not signify a profound change in the role of the state? Does the fact of a government taking a position in a scientific debate not suggest that the state, subject to the pressures of opinion, would like to influence the search for truth and the object of science according to what suits its own interests, in other words, following the direction indicated by public opinion polls? The abandonment of neutrality in this field is only one aspect of the state's gradual privatisation. We understand that a private business owner focuses the research carried out in his laboratories so as to maximise profit and abandons projects that might endanger it. It is more difficult to think that in a democratic regime the theoretical foundations and practical applications of publicly funded research should be dictated by the government according to the opinion of a particularly media-savvy group of citizens.

The clumsiness of certain clinicians, the disappointed hopes, and persistent lack of resources have certainly added to the suffering of families, even though some progress has been made, albeit often limited to specific institutions, where the teams have scrambled to create positions, care institutions, education, and academic integration structures. However, do the current disagreements and attempts at regulation or legislation that are trying to silence these initiatives not imply some larger truth about the direction our society is heading in? Should the question of autism be related to the rise of neoliberalism, to the transformation of the social link, and the dictatorship of opinion associated with it?

The neoliberal society and autism

The chronological coincidences are striking. It was just as Ronald Reagan was taking office in the White House and the neoliberal revolution was beginning that the key journal on autism founded by Kanner, *Journal of Autism and Childhood Schizophrenia*, became the *Journal of Autism and Developmental Disorders*. The psychoanalysts who had been part of its editorial committee were let go; from now on, the journal was only going to publish articles dealing with epidemiology, neuroscience, genetics, and, at times, behaviourist-inspired educational methods. At the same time, a small group working on the revision of the classification of mental disorders at the American Psychiatric Association – a subject of little interest to the majority of its then-members – took over and published the DSM III, a criteria-based, a-theoretical classification, which rejected all references to psychopathology, previously its dominant paradigm. As I have said, the child psychoses disappeared and autism became the new model of a pervasive developmental disorder. President Reagan then only had to suspend the federal funding voted in by the Kennedy administration and effectively kill the previously vibrant "community mental health" programme similar to the French system of "sectors", forcing the parents of autistic children (already little inclined towards a type of psychiatry they saw as blaming them for their child's problems) to turn towards the education system and assert the constitutional right of each child to education. Autism, which was filed under the category of developmental disability together with epilepsy, mental retardation, and cerebral palsy, could then begin its spectacular rise. It was no longer a disease in Kanner's sense, but rather a personality distortion to be corrected using behaviourist methods and, most importantly, a disability providing access to social and academic support. Following the ideology of standardisation, some even argued that specialised support in itself led to marginalisation. By abolishing this stigmatising provision, the society would have to get better at tolerating difference and the disorder would disappear. The cost-cutting logic behind this development is clear. It is less expensive to compensate someone financially for a disability and delegate their care to volunteers than to work to reduce this handicap or prevent it from deteriorating. In this case, public opinion and the need to reduce healthcare costs formed an objective alliance.

Thirty years later, we see the same policy taking shape in France, perhaps in response to the same changing conditions.

The first one is the dictatorship of public opinion. As Pierre Dardot and Christian Laval (2009) explain, our society is now following an entrepreneurial model, which applies equally to public services, private businesses, and individual self-management. Everything is subject to the market and market competition, striving for the optimum cost-benefit ratio. Service users (especially care service users) are increasingly better informed and no longer hire these services on the basis of trust, as it used to be the case in the past. They expect these services, methods, and doctrines to compete with each other, providing evaluations and evidence. Expert opinion no longer carries absolute authority. In the natural sciences, "truth" can still benefit from a certain level of complexity, from its reliance on experimental verification, its generalisable theorems, and the obvious impact that its spectacular results have had on our lives. This explains the success of certain neuroscientists or geneticists, who sometimes announce, not very scrupulously – based on a sparse amount of data obtained under highly specific conditions and from a limited sample – the discovery of an "autism" gene or its link to an issue in a particular region of the cerebral cortex. The humanities are much more fragile and their more debatable observations more difficult to prove. They are also working in fields ruled by folk psychology, folk sociology, or folk economics, which make everyone feel entitled to have an opinion. The close relationship between the observed and the observer, his influence on the way in which data is collected and interpreted, also increase the margin of uncertainty. When trust disappears, expert opinion is more easily opposed with one that is more popular or appears more solid. We only need to remember that Watson, the founder of behaviourist psychology, spent the end of his career in advertising, and we immediately understand that therapies that are inspired by his theory of learning are much better equipped to conquer the market than psychoanalysis and its disturbing "truths". For both electoral and economic reasons, public opinion cajoled by the media imposes itself on political power; the latter, having abandoned its role in regulating, elaborating, transforming, or indeed educating this opinion, now simply relays it. This is very clear in the way the state immediately reacts, by passing new laws, to any collective emotion provoked by a particularly dramatic (and dramatised) piece of news.

In the specific case of autism, the undeniable suffering of families, which reverberates across our screens and in the press, employs another mechanism of the neoliberal society: compassion. Compassion has replaced the social bonds of the past, which were founded on solidarity and the consciousness of being part of a community larger than a simple gathering of individuals. Not so long ago, a victim had a right to compensation; however, in a criminal process it was the social body as a whole that was trying to redress a balance disturbed by the crime or misdemeanour. In today's atomised society, broken down into a multitude of small individual enterprises competing with each other in a struggle for life, the victim is only an individual. Compassion, the immediate interindividual identification with no reference to the collective as a third party, becomes a kind of conditioned reflex when faced with the other's suffering. The suffering of the parents, more visible and easier to express, less distant and strange than that of the child, is the suffering that most resonates in the public realm. Hence the extra value attributed to parental demands. Is anyone still concerned about the needs of the child, initially at the core of the project of the first educators of autists, such as Bruno Bettelheim in the United States or Bernard Durey in France? Has anyone asked an autist what they thought of applied behavioural analysis, or ABA, so appreciated by their parents? (We already know that a movement of persons with Asperger's in Canada has criticised this method as degrading.)

Without trying to be deliberately critical, the attention suddenly paid to this fairly old method (the works of Ingmar Lovaas, who first used it to treat autism, date back to the 1960s) deserves serious examination. Nobody denies the need for education, for autistic children as much as any other child. Nor would anyone deny the need to adapt learning techniques to the child's level of comprehension, sometimes using an ordered system of reinforcing desirable behaviours and avoiding dangerous behaviours or those that damage the relationship to the other. What is problematic is when the advocates and adepts of this method claim that it is the only approach that is effective and evidence-based. The exclusive way in which it is promoted raises the question of the social consensus to which it responds. Consistent with the neoliberal concept of the homogenous, non-conflictual subject, shaped solely by environmental stimuli, its advantages are primarily its absolute lack of concern with the enigmas of psychic life and its common-sense approach. Which pet owner has never spontaneously tried to use a system of rewards and punishments to train their dog or cat? Which parent has not used the same methods to try to make their small child conform to the elementary expectations of their family environment? Its simplicity, the fact that it requires little training and can easily be used by anyone is an excellent marketing strategy. *Do it yourself* is one of the neoliberal society's rules, a society of autonomous entrepreneurs, who are as little dependent on each other as possible. When it is practised according to its rules, the method requires 40 hours per week and a large number of trainers who work in sequence, one-to-one with the child. This high number of interlocutors has the benefit of discouraging any form of transference and thus prevent parents from experiencing dependence (and the ambivalent gratitude that necessarily goes with it), which the neoliberal society considers a sign of weakness. Like any other method focusing purely on observable symptoms, it is also easy to evaluate. As we know, evaluation is another important marketing argument. It therefore seems both erudite and practical, reminding us of the criteria of evidence-based medicine, inspired by comparative studies of antibiotics. At the same time, it responds to one of the key demands of the neoliberal society: short-term efficacy that can be immediately appreciated. It is true that psychoanalysts and other psychopathologists have not been sufficiently concerned with evaluating their highly diverse practices. Behaviourist therapies, on the contrary, have ingeniously made evaluation the centre of their framework, from the very beginning. At the same time, working long-term and trying to facilitate a comprehensive process of growth, psychoanalysts and other relational therapists have found it difficult to measure the effects of their work. It is easier to account for the persisting number of stereotypic behaviours, the frequency of self-harming behaviour or agitation, or the degree of echolalia, than for the individual's pleasure in communicating with others and telling them his story, as well as the quality of wellbeing this exchange engenders.

Échange:[5] a word neoliberalism has little time for, instead preferring "transaction". A transaction is a two-way process. It involves a negotiation between two isolated individuals, two micro-businesses trying to balance their budgets and increase their profits while minimising costs. An exchange necessarily involves a third who guarantees it, a feeling of community and solidarity between the exchanging parties, their shared "human condition", as Montaigne puts it, the source of mutual enrichment. The transacting parties are pre-existing to the act, from which they emerge identical in their being, even though their possessions may have increased or diminished. In an exchange, the individuals are founded by this exchange, they are, as Condillac says, the result of mutual commerce. The idea of autism that seems to dominate today could itself be described as autistic or, at the least, solipsistic. It imagines an isolated individual reduced to a kind of simple machine with a few wheels missing, which must be modified from the outside using supplementary instructions. It is radically opposed to a conception founded on exchange, where progress comes from the inside once certain obstacles have been removed. This removal of an obstacle (*per via di levare*), as Freud argued, does not mean we cannot actively intervene or even provide directions or models; it means that, contrary to the neoliberal paradigm, we see the individual fundamentally as a being in relation, as constructed in and through intersubjectivity. Given that he suffers from a pathology of intersubjectivity, it is difficult to see why the autistic person should be denied this basic human ingredient... unless we give in, once again, to the Sirens of neoliberalism and refuse to recognise him as a thinking being.

And indeed, this is what it ultimately comes down to. Neoliberalism hates thinking. By preferring transaction to exchange, short-term profits to long-term investments, it scorns contemplation, creative dreaming, fantasy, and the poetics of existence. We see this in today's conception of mental health care. From the perspective of market economy that has infiltrated public services (with the state being seen as a kind of private-sector company), psychiatric institutions have to compete on the market and demonstrate not just their efficacy (the quality of the service provided), but also their efficiency, i.e. their ability to provide this service as cheaply as possible. Their new "management" must therefore force each employee to embrace the dominant business model and become, in turn, a little enterprise, subject to performance assessment and incited to do better by a system of sanctions and rewards designed to increase productivity. Hence the management system founded on a chain of surveillance and leading from the general direction to the management of care and to the care centres, from the centres to the services and functional units. The role of middle managers becomes a predominant in the management of "human resources", a system little concerned with the specificity of the tasks managed and easy to transpose to any enterprise providing services or producing consumer goods.

The user, whose power has increased, is no longer considered in terms of the specific ways in which he receives care. He is simply the consumer of a service, the suitability of which to his needs he is the only one to appreciate. He can choose between a number of competing offers. What is called quality assessment is nothing but this idealised power of the user in the larger sense (the patient, his family, the organisations that represent them, but also the funders and authorities that have entrusted the service with its mission, the results of which are assessed by experts and, finally, at the end of the chain, the political power and the electors that sanction it). The increasing ranks of management, at a time when the numbers of frontline staff are being cut, is one of the symptoms of this change. The managers are no longer, or less so, team facilitators. They have become, often against their will, mere agents of surveillance and evaluation. They no longer transmit the results of clinical experience for which they have been promoted, but a generic business model having become an end in itself. The time devoted to evaluation predominates over the evaluated actions themselves. The agenda, what needs to be done, instead becomes the *evaluenda*. Every action is constructed depending on its measurement. We are very far from an understanding of care as an activity aimed at, to use Winnicott's expression, teaching the patient how to play. We are far from the emphasis on free time, time spent solely on the pleasure of thinking, on telling a story, or talking to each other. And equally far from the institutional frameworks trying to encourage the creativity of each practitioner, which used to be a key element of therapy, but has lost value at an age devoted to ready-made methods and care protocols. Resembling each other like car models, with only a few slight differences to seduce the client and gain market share, these protocols are then selected by the type of opinion embodied in the market-like bargaining of the consensus conference.

Here, we should remember that these conferences originated from an organisation typical of the American health care system. In order to curb the skyrocketing costs of healthcare, as part of a thriving and uncontrolled care industry, insurance companies forced their policy holders to enrol in health maintenance organisations, or HMOS. These large chains included doctors, paramedical professionals, and hospitals, competing with each other and listed on the stock exchange. The HMOS organised managed care, i.e. the specification of treatments which the consensus had found to be the most lucrative and most effective for certain "homogenous groups" of patients, and subsequently the only treatments reimbursed. The question of autism, having become a social phenomenon to the extent we have seen in recent years, cannot be easily tackled by this approach, because of the difficulty of fitting the extreme diversity of the autistic spectrum into a homogenous group. Most patients are therefore taken care of by the education system and parents can choose from a small number of duly codified methods competing with each other. The question of whether these methods belong to the healthcare field and should be thus reimbursed by insurance companies or whether they are part of the education system has not been settled in the United States and has been the object of a number of legal disputes.

Conclusion

We indeed do have reasons to worry that, caught between the violent smear campaign, the lack of support, and the often suspicious attitude of the state that employs them, the child psychiatry teams in the public sector might eventually abandon their difficult, ungrateful, and at times discouraging task, which also requires a rare degree of personal investment and devotion. Sparing neither time nor the personal commitment of each of their members, these teams all over the country continue to pursue their work with commendable energy, creativity, and ethics, which the ad-hoc committees seem not to be able to recognise. Yet this type of activism cannot go on forever. We are already hearing voices calling for the desertion from a field where we are allegedly not wanted, in order to deal with other, more gratifying demands, of which there are many. If, as it was the case in the United States, this advice is heeded, it would be a great pity for autists, who will be abandoned to solely operant conditioning and thus lose the hard-won dimension of subjects. It will also be a pity for a certain idea of psychiatry, which would thus abandon its first and founding mission (caring for madness) for the benefit of the rational and neoliberal management of mental health.

Notes

1 The original version of this article was published in *Enfances & Psy*, 46 (1): 15–29.
2 In other words, a comprehensive approach aimed not so much at the "why" but rather the "how".
3 Editors' comments: The shocking revelations about the true nature of Asperger's work and his relationship with the Nazi regime were made public several years after the first publication of this essay by the work of medical historian Herwig Czech of Medical University of Vienna, published in 2018, and were further documented in Edith Sheffer's book *Asperger's Children: The Origins of Autism in Nazi Vienna*, Norton (2018). Also see Yann Diener's chapter in this present collection.
4 Here is an example of the type of messages spread by this organisation: "According to the Department of Health and Human Services, 1 in 91 children –1% of American children – has an autism spectrum disorder. This is a considerable increase from 1 in 150, which was the federal estimate in 2007!"
5 Translator's note: The French *échange* signifies exchange in terms of trade, swapping, as well as dialogue or discussion.

References

Dardot, P. & Laval, C. (2009). *La nouvelle raison du monde, essai sur la société néolibérale*. Paris: La Découverte.

Chapter 2

The lessons of autism

Leonardo S. Rodríguez

Some autistic human beings want psychoanalysis

Among psychoanalysts of the Lacanian movement a principle prevails: we treat our patients – our analysands – "one by one". This principle has the value of an ethical imperative. It emphasises the respect for the patient's singularity, his/her/their being irreducible to just representing "a case of…" – of neurosis, psychosis, autism, or any other diagnostic category. It is both a clinical and an ethical principle, and it is consonant with Lacan's definition of the analyst's desire: a desire "to obtain absolute difference", the opposite of a conception of the aim of analysis as the institution of an identification with the analyst as an ideal, or with any other ideal (Lacan, 1977, p. 276).

In our clinical work, the stress on the singular – as distinct from the universal and the particular, to follow the Aristotelian logical categories – does not mean that in our reflections and conceptual elaborations we can dispense with the reference to universal categories and particular features, signs, and symptoms in the study and actual clinical work with patients, i.e. diagnosis and treatment. The respect for the patient's singularity enables us, and at the same time compels us, to subordinate our diagnostic categories and the orientation of the treatment to the unique experience of the psychoanalytic encounter. The patient may well present traits, signs and symptoms that are typical, if not universal, of a diagnostic category, which in this sense is regarded as a logical class. But the diagnostic indicators that in our perception make the patient "a case of…" are for us only the beginning, not the end, of a collaborative effort between analysand and analyst. It still remains to be learnt, for example, if the patient clearly shows echolalia in his/her/their speech, how the echolalia "works" for the patient, what its function in his/her/their subjective organisation might be, what his/her/their own response to this typical sign is. I write "sign" on purpose, since it is not certain that echolalia (direct or delayed) is a symptom for all autistic patients – "symptom" here understood from a psychoanalytic perspective.

This perspective considers the symptom to be a *production of a subject*, not merely a "disorder" or aberrant deviation; so that in the case of echolalia, for instance, we cannot consider it simply as a disorder or deviation of the function of speech (Rodríguez, 2006).

Given the essential reference in any psychoanalytic study to the structure and functions of the unconscious and the division of the subject, conscious awareness is not a reliable indicator of the existence of a symptom. This is so not only in the case of autistic subjects, but also of any subjects in analysis irrespective of their clinical structure. As a rule, the patient has no clear and distinct idea of what the symptom is really about. At the beginning of the analysis he/she/they is unable to give a correct phenomenological description of the symptom. If he/she/they does, the work of analysis demonstrates that it is a very partial, tendentious and displaced idea, which does not explain its formal presentation or its function *for the subject*. The subject's misrecognition of his/her/their own symptom may even lead to its being completely ignored, as is the case with those symptoms that have become ego-syntonic: instead of producing a disruption for the subject, the subject *adapts* well to the presence and demands imposed by the symptom, which becomes an integral part of his/her/their ego, "character", or "personality".

The autistic subject is a human *subject* in the full sense of the term. That the autistic subject is a *subject of language*, as distinct from being a *subject of the unconscious*, or *desiring subject*, has been a conceptual premise for Lacanian psychoanalysts since Lacan asserted it for cases of psychosis (Cf. "On a question prior to any possible treatment of psychosis"; Lacan, 2006 [1958]). Nowadays some of us have had to revise that premise, as the possibility that the autistic subject be also a *subject of the unconscious* and a *subject of desire*, a *desiring subject*, arises out of paying careful attention to the data of clinical practice. We must at least be prepared to accept that the autistic subject *might be* a subject of the unconscious, even if this formula needs to be qualified for every case. If we rule out the possibility that the patient be capable of desiring, then the direction that we impose to the treatment will restrict our field of operations, and we may end up excluding the signs of the patient's desire on the basis of a false premise.

It may well be the case that the patient's desire is a *creation* of the analysis. This requires that the analyst directs the treatment towards it, which implies that the analyst be convinced that such creation is possible. Some colleagues have spoken in this connection of analyses whose aim is *the production of a subject* – a modality of treatment that still regards the subject in analytic treatment as a subject of language, but not a subject of the unconscious or desiring subject at the beginning of the treatment. In this perspective, the analytic discourse retains its structural arrangement: at the locus of the *production* the S_1 represents the signifier with which the autistic subject may enter ordinary discourse as a desiring subject.

$$\frac{a}{S_2} \to \frac{\$}{S_1}$$

Experience shows that the insertion of an autistic subject into ordinary discourse has its limitations. Yet the testimony of those human beings who have been capable of entering social life and contribute to it, sometimes in very creative ways, suggests that what they have achieved spontaneously, using their own means and without analytic treatment, can serve as a useful reference for the psychoanalyst, in a way analogous to the inspiration obtained from the creations and inventions of psychotic writers, artists, and scientists (Grandin, 2005; Sellin, 1995; Williams, 1992, 1994). The follow-up studies of Leo Kanner refer to creative and/or inventive outcomes for a number of patients (Kanner, 1973). On the question of the *psychotic's* capacity for invention, Lacan exposed some views in his seminar on the *sinthome* that are pertinent in discussing the treatment of autistic patients. In the same volume of the seminar, there are relevant remarks by its editor, Jacques-Alain Miller (Lacan, 2016, pp. 110–111, 132, 193).

We also have the testimonies of autistic subjects who have been through the psychoanalytic experience and who have been transformed by it. On the other hand, some of our autistic patients have not benefitted from the experience in a significant way – although in my experience no autistic patient has finished the psychoanalytic treatment without some gain. The same finding applies to the family of the patient. The family of the patient as a rule provides the primary carers of the patient, and theirs can be a task and a responsibility that impose demands that the community as a whole does not always recognise.

In psychoanalysis we are familiar with unfavourable outcomes of clinical psychoanalysis with patients of *all* clinical structures. We have learnt a few things from our mistakes, and from experiences that have turned out to be unproductive but whose outcome cannot be attributed to identifiable mistakes of either the analyst or the patient. Certainly, we cannot claim to have radically cured any autistic patient, in the sense of having produced a fundamental subjective change specified by the removal of his/her/their autism. It could be argued that such an outcome (removal of the pathological manifestations of a clinical structure) is only possible in the case of neurotics – a debatable point that is outside the limits of this study. But the psychoanalytic treatment of a considerable number of autistic patients from all around the world has produced verifiable improvements in the lives of patients and those directly concerned and affected by the patient's states: family, friends, teachers, and other workers. We regard autism as first and foremost a *subjective position* rather than a nosological entity. As a subjective position, like all other positions that subjects come to occupy in human life, autism may generate self-destructiveness and suffering; but not only self-destruction and suffering, as there are autistic subjects who are as happy and constructive as any human being can be; and this, despite the response of others who are not prepared to tolerate the autistic human subject's idiosyncratic approach to human relations, their eccentricities, and their lack of insertion or unusual form of insertion in the social bonds of ordinary discourse.

What we know about autism from a psychoanalytic perspective derives from clinical experience, which is regularly prompted by troubled situations that involve suffering. It is also some form of trouble that has taken autistic people to the care of other specialists – in the fields of education, occupational guidance, and a number of chapters of medicine. What the autistic subject regards as trouble and what his/her/their significant others regard as trouble are two different things. Typically, what the autistic patient regards as trouble are the demands by others that he/she/they behave according to the expectations of ordinary discourse and the established rules of conventional institutions and social engagement, even if the patient does not actively act against those expectations and rules. The autistic patient also regards as trouble alterations imposed by others in his/her/their immediate *Umwelt*, the space arranged according to the laws of the imaginary order (in the Lacanian sense of a register of human experience), which in autism tends to be marked by a rigid requirement of sameness. The others consider that the patient is in trouble if he/she/they does not comply with the "normal" expectations and rules, even if the non-compliance does not cause any harm to anybody. For some people, the non-compliance with social expectations is tolerable, but they are perhaps a minority. I have known quite a few autistic subjects who are docile and very compliant when ordered to perform productive (i.e. socially productive) tasks of which they are capable. For some non-autistic fellow human beings this is quite acceptable; but for others that is not so, as the tasks involved are restricted, and usually (but not always) repetitive, and the inability of the autistic subjects to engage in occupations or courses of study that are different from their preferred ones is arbitrarily regarded as antisocial. That the inability to engage in a good number of specific occupations is a *universal* feature of human beings is not taken into account for those intolerant fellow human beings who are adversely sensitive to particular versions of the universal human lack-in-being. As for the perception of alterations into one's *Umwelt*, or imaginary order, the rejection of the intrusions of others into one's space (the body and its surroundings) is virtually universal – the difference between autistic people and others being that they prefer their own idiosyncratic arrangements. Now, there are plenty of non-autistic idiosyncratic arrangements of the ways people deal with their bodies, their personal appearance, and the spaces where they live and work.

In my own practice I have followed the rule that I only receive the patient if the patient wants to see me and, if the patient is a child, he/she tells a parent that they want to see me – as a child is dependent on a caring adult to come to consult an analyst. In my work with autistic people, I have been encouraged by the fact that most of the autistic patients I have seen over the years have clearly expressed the wish to see me, or at least have not opposed coming to analysis – including cases of children who had refused other forms of social contact and who have not wanted to visit other practitioners. I have thought that *something within them* propelled them to come to visit an analyst, even before meeting the analyst for the first time: ostensibly, on the basis of a persuasive approach by their parents who spoke specifically about the analyst and what an analyst does – as I requested the parents to do in our initial contact. That *something* is of the order of desire, however "timid" or "soft" this might be. This is an ethical, and not only a conceptual and technical question: it is not easy to establish clinically, although not impossible, whether an autistic patient's desire is engaged in the experience. The rationale for the treatment of autistic patients that involve the *production* of a *desiring subject* implies that a desiring subject is absent at the beginning of the treatment. Autistic subjects are not the only patients in such a subjective position: the cases of some psychotic patients can also be understood along similar lines, and even in cases of neurosis it is not infrequent that the patient's desire is not engaged in the transference relation and the work of analysis for a good part of the treatment.

A desire already at work in the initial phase of the treatment has been present in my clinical experience with a number of young autistic patients who articulated a wish to come to see me after the first session or after a reduced number of sessions. In all those cases their parents told me that this was the first time in their lives that those children expressed a positive wish of *any* kind. Is it that an analyst's disposition and readiness to listen to and to work with an autistic subject without demanding anything finds a receptive ear in someone who ostensibly shows no interest in others?

On the other hand, it was only after years of analytic labour that some other autistic children and adolescents were able, for the first time in their lives, to speak for themselves and express demands and wishes consonant with the emergence of a *real desire*. I use this expression ("a real desire") deliberately, in the sense of *a desire in the order of the real*, which is possible only if the symbolic and imaginary frameworks that sustain human desire are in place, limited as they might be for the patient.

An autistic eight-year-old boy with very limited intellectual capacity showed the typical signs of autism described by Leo Kanner (Kanner, 1973 [1943]), and for years our work showed no indication that one day he would be able to "come out" of his autistic aloofness and echolalic verbal production. Yet he and I persisted with our analytic work, and eventually he could employ speech to speak for himself, in a rudimentary yet clear way. He approached others, including myself, with requests that were his own, not echolalic, not stereotypical, grounded in his limited interhuman experiences and taking into account the Other's desire as a reference point. He would then tell me about his troubles at school, his impotence in dealing with a rejecting father, and his sense of guilt for tormenting his mother. He has remained a very restricted social being from a conventional point of view; yet he is now capable of engaging his subjectivity and his incipient desire with those who are prepared to share a portion of their own lives with him: his mother, his sister, his teachers, and other workers that have accompanied him in the adventure of humanisation.

The lessons that we have gained from the experience with autistic subjects have helped us to learn about human functions that are present in everybody. The marked contrast between autistic and all other subjects in relation to those functions is highly instructive for our understanding of the workings of the unconscious, of language and discourse, of the imaginary and symbolic representation of the body, and of affective life – and a few other questions of psychoanalytic interest.

The diagnostic question: psychoanalysis and psychiatry

In my clinical experience (and the experience of other fellow psychoanalysts), there is by and large agreement between what we, psychoanalysts, regard as diagnostically structural features of autism and the criteria employed by other workers, in particular psychiatrists. The differences between the psychoanalyst and other workers arise when it is a question of applying the knowledge gained in the diagnostic phase of the treatment.

There is a vast amount of literature on autism, mainly from researchers in psychiatry, the neurosciences, and education. The number of available texts in psychoanalysis is much more modest; but there have been a few original contributions that are worth studying. Autism is not a favourite topic among psychoanalysts, and the number of psychoanalysts who have clinical experience with autistic patients is very restricted. The treatment of an autistic patient requires not only patience but, more importantly, a creative effort so as to find a way to gain access to the patient's subjectivity. Our usual technical instruments have to be adapted to exceptional situations, and a degree of inventiveness is required for an experience that renders the psychoanalyst, as our friend the late Vicente Mira put it, frequently confined to "not doing anything and not knowing what to do". The condition is not radically curable; yet clinical experience shows that, as it happens with many other pathological conditions, autism is treatable, and that to autistic patients and their families the analytic treatment makes quite a difference.

When we discuss autism, we usually refer to *autistic children*. In due course autistic children become autistic adults; but our culture – our professional culture of services provided to people, as well as our culture at large – tends to forget that autistic *adults* are still autistic. The result is that after the age of 18 or so the autistic patient is left in a diagnostic and treatment limbo. He tends to be diagnosed as suffering from an atypical form of schizophrenia, or as being intellectually disabled, or as having an antisocial personality disorder; or some other diagnosis that is of no practical help to the patient or to their family, with the tragic consequences of social segregation. Referring to "him", rather than "him or her" is pertinent, as most autistic patients are male – the estimates speak of 80% of cases, although there are significant variations in the estimates in different areas: from 2:1 to 15:1 (boys to girls ratio).

There is no prevailing doctrine as to the aetiology of autism. The studies on contributing factors range from the developmental, psychiatric, neurologic, and chromosomal to the genetic. The 1950s and 1960s emphasis on maternal neglect and a supposed "refrigerated" approach to the infant is no longer accepted, even if for us, psychoanalysts, questions concerning the mother's and father's desire continue to be pertinent.

There has been a substantial increase in the number of patients diagnosed with autism by psychiatrists, psychologists, and paediatricians. Professor Pamela Campbell, of Southern Illinois University, has reported the statistical estimates of the prevalence of autism reproduced below (Campbell, 2019):

- Kanner's estimate 150:20,000
- 1966 estimate at 4–5:10,000 (1:1,000)
- 1970 formal prevalence study found 4–5:10,000

The Autism and Developmental Monitoring Network (USA) has reported:

- 2002: 1:150
- 2004: 1:125
- 2006: 1:110
- 2008: 1:88
- 2012: 1:68

In Australia there has been a reasonably reliable system of detection of autism in children of kindergarten age (three and four years old), and an increase in the incidence of autism has also been reported.

This increase in prevalence has been interpreted by some practitioners as an effect of the expansion of the corresponding diagnostic category in the two dominant nosological classifications (the DSM-5 and the ICD-10), now entitled *autism spectrum disorders*. It is possible that the actual number of autistic subjects has increased, if we retain the diagnostic criteria that prevailed until not so long ago and that still remain the clinical guidelines for psychoanalysts – not for all psychoanalysts, but at least for those of us who follow the teachings of Freud, Lacan, and a few other leading authors in our discipline and in psychiatry. The first editions of the DSM did not include a separate category for childhood autism, and regarded autism as a form of early schizophrenia. Until not so long ago, a few colleagues still regarded infantile autism as the earliest form of schizophrenia; and some contemporary colleagues, like Pierre Bruno, a Lacanian psychoanalyst, still (or at least 20 years ago) regard the structures of autism and schizophrenia as identical (cf. my comment on this point in *Psychoanalysis with Children*; Rodríguez, 1999).

The criteria for early childhood autism that we still employ are those established by Leo Kanner in 1943, although some of the signs and features that Kanner described require some qualifications on our part. The contemporary psychiatric classifications of the American Psychiatric Association (the DSM-5) and the World Health Organization (the ICD-10) have only partially retained Kanner's criteria, the result being in my opinion a less precise diagnostic picture, with the omission of the characteristic signs of autism concerning language and discourse and a misleading description of intellectual functioning in autistic subjects.

Kanner's diagnostic criteria are still valid, if some precision is introduced in his assessment of the peculiar features of language and discourse in autistic subjects. They comprise eight main features: (i) the inability to relate socially; (ii) aloofness; (iii) the failure to assume an anticipatory posture; (iv) a profound disturbance of language; (v) the presence of excellent rote memory in many cases; (vi) echolalia and delayed echolalia; (vii) literalness; and (viii) the mechanical repetition of pronouns.

The points that in our view require revision are iv, vi, vii, and viii, all of which concern language and discourse. Kanner was right in identifying the functions involved, but he did not have at his disposal the advances in linguistics of the last few decades, in particular the studies on the pragmatics of language and on language acquisition. Nevertheless, his clinical observations, including those that involve linguistic functions directly, published in his original paper of 1943 and in the papers on his follow-up studies are still very valuable.

Kanner was not a psychoanalyst and was not particularly sympathetic to the contributions that the psychoanalysts of the 1940s and 1950s offered to the understanding of autism. But he interpreted the clinical signs of autism from a perspective that agrees with the psychoanalytic approach; namely, that those clinical signs must be regarded as *productions* and *inventions* of the patient, rather than mere deficits. He followed up the group of patients whose cases he reported in his 1943 paper, and pointed out in his follow-up studies that some of the patients, while remaining autistic, had developed intellectual and practical skills that enabled them to enter the social circuit, whereas those patients who did not present the positive autistic signs (mannerisms, repetitive behaviours, peculiar forms of speech, etc.) that they had exhibited in 1943 had entered into states of involution and loss of the intellectual and affective functions that they had ten or 20 years earlier. His interpretation was that their autistic signs and features were achievements and contributed to their mental stabilisation, even if they appeared to be bizarre and profoundly deviated from the prevailing norms for mental health. His clinical approach was in agreement with clinical psychoanalysis: he interpreted symptomatic formations and signs as *productions* rather than *deficits* – deficits that are usually described as the mere absence or lack of achievement of human functions regarded as universally necessary. Kanner writes in his paper, "Follow-up studies of eleven autistic children originally reported in 1943":

> The results we have obtained do not lend themselves to statistical considerations due to the reduced number of cases involved. On the other hand, they invite to pose serious questions about the spectrum of

evolutions, which go from complete deterioration to professional adaptation associated with limited but superficially good social adaptation.

(Kanner, 1973)

After Kanner

A few psychoanalysts and psychoanalytic psychotherapists of the neo-Kleinian movement, like Donald Meltzer and Frances Tustin, and others trained in the ego psychology tradition in the United States, like Margaret Mahler, worked with autistic patients and published a few original ideas.

In Lacanian psychoanalysis, the impetus to clinical work and research on autism was inspired by the work of Rosine and Robert Lefort, which extended from the early 1950s until the first years of this century. The analysis of Marie-Françoise by Rosine Lefort, discussed at length in *The Birth of the Other* (1980), and reviewed by the Leforts in their last publication, *La distinction de l'autisme* (2003), has been inspirational to those of us who work with autistic patients. Lacan himself left only a few, but significant reflections on or relevant to autism – in particular his Geneva lecture on the symptom (cf. *Analysis* No. 1) and his *Seminar XXIII*, on the sinthome.

I can only refer concisely to a selected number of authors who have produced original contributions on autism in Lacanian psychoanalysis. They have all developed separate aspects of the clinical and theoretical questions relevant to autism. Put together, they do not amount to a coherent or consistent theory, but constitute nevertheless a set of positive findings and plausible conceptual elaborations.

We must bear in mind that, unlike all the other fundamental clinical questions in psychoanalysis that have been the object of research and conceptual debate since Freud, and which therefore may be regarded as "Freudian" questions, autism was not a Freudian question. It became a question for Lacan rather late in his life, and Lacan did not leave us with any specific conceptual guidelines, as he did with the psychoses, the neuroses, and the perversions.

In their book, *La distinction de l'autisme* (*The distinction of autism*), and apropos the case of Marie-Françoise, Rosine and Robert Lefort discuss four central clinical features of the autistic syndrome (Lefort & Lefort, 2003). They refer to autism as a *syndrome* (i.e. a group of symptoms that occur together consistently), but also pose the question as to whether autism should not be considered as a separate clinical structure, or fourth structure alongside the neuroses, the perversions, and the psychoses. As such, it could perhaps be specified by a modality of *foreclosure* that could include, but would not be limited to, the foreclosure of the Name-of-the-father. The extension of such mechanism would still be identified. Now, in favour of such a hypothesis is the clinical observation that in autism the subjective registration of signifiers is as a whole compromised, for reasons that are still to be elucidated.

The four clinical features proposed by the Leforts are:

(i) a drive to destruction and self-destruction manifested in the patient's violence.

This dominance of destruction/self-destruction is the basis of the relation of the autistic subject with the external world, in relation to which he remains a complete stranger, and which constitutes for him an intolerable threat of intrusion.
(Lefort & Lefort, 2003, p. 14, my translation)

(ii) The fundamental aetiological point of such structure is that for the autistic subject there is no Other. This is evident in the transference relation, where the analyst does not exist qua Other, be it the Other of the image, the Other of the signifier or the Other as holder of the object. The Leforts elaborate on the consequences of the absence of the Other for the constitution of the drive itself and of the real objects of the world.
(iii) The double: the absence of the Other means the absence of the hole in the Other and of the signifier of the lack in the Other; these absences make of the double a fundamental and structural component of autism. The absence of the signifier of the Other excludes identifications. In the absence of the Other as mediator, there is no relation between an $i(a)$ and an $i'(a)$, so that the link is between two $i(a)$. The division of the subject takes place in the real of the double – in the real of the same. The real image (as distinct from the *virtual* image) does not enable the access to the specular order, which makes possible the linking of the image of the body with the object a. The latter derives from the field of the Other and creates an alterity, but not the uncanny experience of the double.
iv) The mirror in the real: the absence of the image in the autistic subject, in whom the double comes to occupy the place permanently, has a radical consequence, which is the absence of the specular order as such.

The Leforts discuss the peculiar phenomena of language and discourse in autism, but their interest in this crucial feature is more limited. They write:

One of the aspects that have enabled us to define the autistic structure is evidently the relation that the autistic subject has with speech and language. It is known that the mute autistic subject is one of the most striking images, but it is far from being the norm. Eight of the eleven children that Kanner followed up acquired the possibility of speaking at the usual age or with some delay. Three children remain mute.

The relation with language is, to begin with, dominated by echolalia and the confusion affecting personal pronouns.
(Lefort & Lefort, 2003, p. 44)

Other researchers have attributed more significance to the peculiar approaches to language and discourse among autistic subjects.

Marie-Christine Laznik, a colleague who works in Paris and has conducted extensive research on the relations between autistic children and their mothers in the context of a large multidisciplinary study, has highlighted the impact of the autistic process on the development of the circuit of the drives, particularly the scopic and the invocatory drives, and how that circuit is interrupted, which causes the isolation of both infant and mother from each other and the institution of an autistic circuit. Some of her papers have been published in English by the *Journal of the Centre for Freudian Analysis and Research*, and there are a few video tapes of her talks and interviews with patients on YouTube (Laznik, 1992, 2008, 2009, 2014).

Pierre Bruno, on whose perspective I commented in my book on analysis with children, postulates the identity of structure between schizophrenia and autism on the basis of the absence of the *subject of the enunciation* in both of them (Bruno, 1992, 1993; Rodríguez, 1999). This is correlative of echolalia as a major diagnostic indicator: the subject can only repeat the verbal productions of an Other that lacks the essential properties of the Other of ordinary discourse as treasure of the signifier, as site of the lack in representation (and therefore of desire), and as non-existent *qua* guarantor of jouissance and knowledge. The echolalic repetition of words rules, disregarding the requirements of life and the social context.

Colette Soler agrees with Bruno as to the essential diagnostic value of the absence of the subject of the enunciation, but does not agree with the postulate of an identity of structure between autism and schizophrenia (Soler, 1990; Rodríguez, 1999).

Jean-Claude Maleval is well known for his studies on the psychoses. In 2009 he published two books: the first is a collection of articles by different authors that he edited, under the title *L'autiste, son double et ses objets* (Maleval at al., 2009), and the second is his own, *L'autiste et sa voix* (Maleval, 2009). Both volumes are very interesting. The collective book has articles on the history and contemporary developments on autism; the question of the double in autism; autistic objects; clinical cases and problems; and a final section on questions of differential diagnosis: autism versus schizophrenia.

Maleval's own book deals with, firstly, a historical overview of the progression from the conception of autism as the earliest form of schizophrenia to the notion of a diagnostic spectrum. Then it deals with the development of language in autism, with particular reference to the deficiencies in babbling and *lalangue*. The third section is a study of jouissance in autism, with references to the double, what the author calls "complex autistic objects" and the "pockets" of competent performance and the attempts to constitute what he calls "an Other of synthesis". There follows a section on the question of hallucinations in autistic subject; a fifth on different modalities of treatment, and a final commentary on education, under the subtitle of "Learning is not enough". I cannot comment here on these rich and vast series of studies that incorporate the findings and proposals of the other authors I have mentioned.

Over the last ten years I have been interested in the questions posed by the concept and clinic of *lalangue*, and have found Maleval's reference to it very instructive despite its brevity, and his discussion of the responses to "baby talk", or *motherese*, by autistic infants, as well as studies outside psychoanalysis but highly relevant to our research on the voice and the different material modalities of verbal communication in autistic and non-autistic children. In 2001, in a paper on autistic speech, I discussed the conceptual foundations and clinical manifestations of the diagnostic criteria proposed by Kanner that involve language, speech, and discourse directly – namely, the questions of the disturbance of language; the so called "literalness", and the mechanical repetition of pronouns (Rodríguez, 2001). In that study there was no reference to the concept and phenomenology of *lalangue* and other aspects of the pragmatics of discourse. But the paper contains some conclusions that are still valid, I believe, and which concern the pragmatics of discourse and the implications for clinical practice. In a 2012 paper on discourse and *lalangue* I referred to the interest that the latter concept (which Lacan developed in the 1970s and which is still work-in-progress) has, among other things, for our understanding of the status of language, speech, and discourse in autism. Autism follows a failure in the establishment of *lalangue*, the material basis of language and of the first modality of human discourse: typically, the *motherese*, that dialectal form of language that a mother and her infant co-create (cf. recent studies on language acquisition; among others, Kuhl (2000) and Cristophe et al., 2009, as well as Darian Leader's essay on the voice; Leader, 2003).

I have found it useful to organise the study of clinical practice and the direction of a treatment itself, according to the four parameters proposed by Lacan (see also Rosine and Robert Lefort's introduction to their book, *La distinction de l'autisme*; Lefort & Lefort, 2003): $, S_1, S_2, a, to which the i (a) proposed by the Rosine and Robert Lefort should be added.

The features common to all autistic subjects are, in my view: (a) Echolalia, more or less extending to all forms of discourse, but always present in relation to a significant subjective engagement of the subject. (b) The subject of the enunciation is phenomenologically absent, and this occurs even in instances in which the subject is capable of saying "I" or "you" correctly; but he/she/they does so mechanically – echolalically. This appears in the psychoses in different degrees, more clearly in schizophrenia than in paranoia, but is also present in paranoia. In this sense, the autistic subject, like the psychotic, is *outside discourse*. The *deictic* function of speech is affected seriously, and as a consequence the subject cannot speak for himself, i.e. from his/her/their own subjective position. He/she/they speak from the position of an Other which, in the absence of the subject, does not really exist (on the deictic function and the related topic of performative speech, see Austin, 1962; Benveniste, 1971;

Rodríguez, 2001). This autistic Other that does not exist is non-existent in a sense different from the Other that does not exist in the case of the neurotic and the "normal" unconscious – that is, an Other that does not exist *qua* guarantor of truth and desire and reliable site of jouissance; the autistic subject is restricted to being an object in a world of objects without subject, other or Other. (c) Absence of equivocity in speech, at the three levels of equivocity (homophonic, grammatical, logical. Cf. Lacan, 2001 [1973]), and therefore absence of jokes and metaphor, poetic or other forms of metaphor, and therefore no "proper" conversion symptoms. (d) No interest in the mirror image, or in the image of the other's body. The phenomenon of the double, which replaces the attraction for the specular image, may well be universal – this remains to be verified.

In consonance with the principle that the creation of desire is possible with autistic subjects, in the analysis of an autistic patient it is possible to create the foundations for the instauration of the subject of the enunciation, the insertion in ordinary discourse, the capacity to apprehend the equivocity of words and larger verbal expressions, and the acquisition of a critical perception of the double. This cannot be promised to every patient and his/her/their family, but it cannot be excluded for any case either.

The clinical experience

What follows is a brief discussion of a few cases of autistic subjects that I have come to know very well, some of whom were, or have been, in treatment for years, as I have continued to work with them after their childhood and adolescence.

B, first known at age four, clearly autistic at that stage and probably since the first year of life. I worked with him until he turned 18, when he and his family moved to another country. He presented delayed echolalia, and he retained this symptom until our last session, although the content of his repeated words changed from time to time, with preservation of some favourite topics. At first, his speech was logorrhea without punctuation, and virtually unintelligible. After a few weeks I realised that what he said were the texts of commercials from the television, which fascinated him. The television set appeared to occupy the place of his Other. He demanded that it be permanently switched on. He was not interested in any particular show, but only in the commercial advertisements – which normally present themselves as fairly echolalic. With time I noticed that he was specially fascinated by the advertisements that involved cars. Over the years he developed an extraordinary memory for cars: models, components, countries of origin. I gained the impression that he knew all the brands and models of all cars around the world. He appeared to have hallucinatory experiences, as I observed many times that he responded in a low voice to statements of someone not really present. He also developed an extraordinary memory for numbers and the results of football matches. Again, I gained the impression that he remembered the results of all matches in the whole history of Australian Rules football. His memory involved signifiers devoid of contextual sense, although they appeared to have some form of meaning for him. As he grew, he learnt at school a few formulas used in social exchanges, and repeated them outside their contextual frame. For years there was no subject of the enunciation in his verbalisations: he was an object among objects, to use the Leforts' characterisation. He adopted a rather rigid imaginary posture, but not excessively so. He attended high school with special assistance, and eventually found a rather mechanical clerical job at which he was diligent and extremely reliable. He was generally a very happy human being, who became annoyed only when others demanded that he did things that he found incomprehensible. He learnt to play a musical instrument and was fairly competent at it. He had an excellent music teacher with experience with autistic, psychotic, and intellectually disabled people. On a limited scale, he was then able to speak for himself and to express his desire. He was able to address demands to me – demands that are absent in subjects who are completely echolalic.

M, treated between the ages of ten and 17: his autism was secondary to a known neurological disorder that is commonly accompanied by autistic signs and features. He was intellectually capable of quite a few tasks, but nevertheless he had limited cognitive skills and very poor perception of human relations, which was aggravated by his totalitarian attitude towards others. He was not as happy as other autistic patients, was usually in a bad mood, and very impatient and intolerant if not understood – and he made no particular effort at being understood. He could not comprehend why I had not watched the entire series of the *Star Wars* movies, or why I was not a supporter of the Collingwood Football Club – he was positively annoyed by my ignorance. He had compulsive routines and fixed ideas – his echolalia was manifest as prejudices and stereotypical expressions repeated at the first occasion. He also had an extraordinary memory for nonsensical material: results of sport events and dates and places that he had never visited. He was able to become partially inserted in discourse as subject of the enunciation, and he was not an object among objects. He adopted a rigid imaginary posture, but not typically autistic – as many psychotic and non-psychotic people occasionally exhibit.

P, from the age of nine, and still in treatment at 19. He initially presented as intellectually handicapped, with extreme inhibitions, fixations, and delusional persecutory formations, and stereotypical superstitions. The function of the subject of the enunciation was not absent in him, but it was extremely reduced. His posture was and has remained rigid. He has developed some artistic talent and has been able to enter into limited but meaningful dialogue concerning some aspects of his life – not only with me but also with other people.

T, seen over 30 years since the age of four, nowadays only sporadically. He has remained illiterate and echolalic, and his speech is marked by the perseveration (repetitive fixations) of phrases and questions. There is no apparent subject of the enunciation. Yet he is an excellent worker in a job that does not require many skills, but which demands dedication and a degree of concentration, and has been able to express his desire in a limited way in the work setting as well as in his family life.

R, four years old, exhibited what he called his "writing" from the moment of our first encounter – a form of representation that could be called "graphic delayed echolalia". He developed precociously an excellent reading ability: he learnt to read at the age of three, all by himself, according to his parents. He had a hyperfixation on texts; extraordinary visual and textual memory (maps, texts of short stories); no subject of the enunciation; postural flexibility subordinated to the textual fixation.

Clinical and ethical questions

The autistic subject, him/her/themself object among objects, is easily treated as an object by others (cf. Lacan's "Note on the child"; Lacan, 1990a; Rodríguez, 1993, 2008, 2017). His subjectivity is thus obliterated by people, institutions and educational programmes that have the best intentions for him. Institutions and families tend to assume legal and practical responsibility for what appears to be a non-existent sense of subjective ethical responsibility, along the lines established by the law for those who are "legally insane".

How to respect the subjectivity of the autistic subject while at the same time respecting his singularity, which entails a very "atypical" uniqueness, a uniqueness outside discourse, and also outside reasonable (i.e. not purely arbitrary) requirements of social life? At this point the limits – the impasse and impotence – of conventional discourse becomes evident. Psychoanalysis is a practice grounded on the respect for uniqueness, but this is possible only within the limits imposed by discourse itself. Psychoanalysis is indeed an experience of discourse, "one of the few still viable for us" (Lacan, 1990b). The encouragement to speak and create a social bond that the fundamental rule of psychoanalysis (and the technical alterations required by each case) promotes necessarily imposes limits, without which there is no sustainable social bond. The parameters set by what has become "typical" in the psychoanalytic experience of discourse should not operate as constraints. The creativity and inventiveness of the psychoanalyst is here required – as it is indeed required in the analysis of anyone, whatever the clinical structure in which she/he/they is situated.

References

American Psychiatric Association (2013). *Diagnostic and Statistical Manual of Mental Disorders. Fifth Edition (DSM-5)*. Washington, DC and London: American Psychiatric Publishing.

Austin, J.L. (1962). *How to Do Things with Words*. Oxford: Oxford University Press.
Benveniste, É. (1971). *Problems in General Linguistics*. Coral Gables: University of Miami Press.
Bruno, P. (1993). Schizophrénie et paranoïa. *Préliminaire*, 5, 67–83.
Bruno, P. *et al.* (1992). *L'autisme et la psychanalyse*. Toulouse: Presses Universitaires du Mirail.
Campbell, P. (2019). *The Clinical Diagnosis of Autism: Are We Over Diagnosing?* Springfield, IL: Neuroscience Institute, Southern Illinois University School of Medicine. www.illinoisaap.org/wp-content/uploads/A32.pdf.
Cristophe, A., Friederici, A., Mampe, B. & Wermke, K. (2009). Newborn's cry melody is shaped by their native language. *Current Biology*, 19(23).
Grandin, T. (2005). *Thinking in Pictures: My Life with Autism*. New York: Vintage Books.
Kanner, L. (1973 [1943]). Autistic disturbances of affective contact. In *Childhood Psychosis: Initial Studies and New Insights*. Washington, DC: Winston & Sons, 1–43.
Kanner, L. (1973 [1955]). Notes on the follow-up studies of autistic children. In *Childhood Psychosis: Initial Studies and New Insights*. Washington, DC: Winston & Sons, 77–90.
Kanner, L. (1973). Follow-up study of eleven autistic children originally reported in 1943. In *Childhood Psychosis: Initial Studies and New Insights*. Washington, DC: Winston & Sons, 161–188.
Kuhl, P.K. (2000). A new view of language acquisition. *Proceedings of the National Academy of Sciences of the United States of America* [PNAS], 97(22), 11850–11857.
Lacan, J. (1977). *The Four Fundamental Concepts of Psycho-Analysis*. London: Tavistock.
Lacan, J. (1988a). *The Seminar, Book I, Freud's Papers on Technique, 1953–1954*. Cambridge: Cambridge University Press.
Lacan, J. (1989). Geneva lecture on the symptom. *Analysis*, 1, 7–26.
Lacan, J. (1990a). Note on the child. *Analysis*, 2, 7–8.
Lacan, J. (1990b). *Television*. New York: Norton.
Lacan, J. (2001 [1973]). L'étourdit. In *Autres écrits*. Paris: Seuil.
Lacan, J. (2006 [1958]). On a question prior to any possible treatment of psychosis. In *Écrits*, New York and London: Norton.
Lacan, J. (2016). *The Seminar, Book XXIII, The Sinthome*. Cambridge: Polity Press.
Laznik, M.C. (2008). Rhythm, presence, voice, breath – bearing witness to Lacan's handling of the transference. *Journal of the Centre for Freudian Analysis and Research*, 18.
Laznik, M.C. (2009). The Lacanian theory of the drive: an examination of possible gains for research in autism. *Journal of the Centre for Freudian Analysis and Research*, 19, 41–62.
Laznik, M.C. (2014). Psychoanalytic treatment of a two month old baby with an autistic brother, showing warning signs of a similar development. *Journal of the Centre for Freudian Analysis and Research*, 25, 16–47.
Laznik, M.C. (1992) Du ratage de la mise en place de l'image du corps au ratage de la mise en place du circuit pulsionnel, quand l'aliénation fait défaut. In P. Alerini *et al.*, *La clinique de l'autisme: son enseignement psychanalytique*. Paris: Point Hors Ligne.
Leader, D. (2003). The voice as psychoanalytic object. *Analysis*, 12, 70–82.

Lefort, R. & Lefort, R. (1984). L'enfant: un analysant à part entière. *L'Âne*, 16, 3–5.
Lefort, R. & Lefort, R. (1991). *Schéma optique et structures, avec référence à la psychose et à l'autisme*. Paper presented at the Centre for Psychoanalytic Research, Melbourne, on 22 April 1991.
Lefort, R. & Lefort, R. (1992). Autisme et psychose. Deux signifiants: "partie" et "cassé". In P. Bruno*et al.*, *L'autisme at la psychanalyse*. Toulouse: Presses Universitaires du Mirail.
Lefort, R. & Lefort, R. (1994). *Birth of the Other*. Urbana and Chicago: Illinois University Press.
Lefort, R. & Lefort, R. (2003). *La Distinction de l'autisme*. Paris: Seuil.
Maleval, J.-C. (2009). *L'autiste et sa voix*. Paris: Seuil.
Maleval, J.-C.*et al.* (2009). *L'autiste, son double et ses objets*. Rennes: Presses Universitaires de Rennes.
Rodríguez, L. (1993). At the limits of the transference: psychoanalysis and autism. *Analysis*, 4, 73–76.
Rodríguez, L. (1999). *Psychoanalysis with Children*. London and New York: Free Association Books.
Rodríguez, L. (2001). Autistic speech. *Analysis*, 10, 124–136.
Rodríguez, L. (2006). Diagnosis in psychoanalysis. *Web Journal of the Centre for Freudian Analysis and Research*.
Rodríguez, L. (2008). Autistic transference. *Journal of the Centre for Freudian Analysis and Research*, 18.
Rodríguez, L. (2012). Discourse and lalangue. *Analysis*, 18, 151–166.
Rodríguez, L. (2017). Psychoanalysis with children, the work with parents and the clinical structures. In C. Owens and S. Farrelly Quinn (Eds.), *Lacanian Psychoanalysis with Babies, Children, and Adolescents: Further Notes on the Child*. London: Karnac.
Sellin, B. (1995). *I Don't Want to Be Inside Me Anymore*. New York: Basic Books.
Soler, C. (1990). Hors discours: autisme et paranoïa. *Les feuillets psychanalytiques du Courtil*, 2, 9–24.
Williams, D. (1992). *Nobody Nowhere*. New York: Perennial.
Williams, D. (1994). *Somebody Somewhere*. New York: Three Rivers Press.

Chapter 3

Like the monotonous voice of the *gusle*

Some reflections on autism[1]

Graciela Prieto

For some time, the pseudoscientific ideology advocating a purely bio-genetic causality of "mental illness", especially autism, has been gaining in strength. Under the influence of powerful pharmaceutical, commercial, and parental lobbies, and supposedly speaking in the name of scientific discoveries, this evolving discourse has argued that the psychoanalytic approach to autism is untenable. In this text, I would like to examine the ways in which this ideology contorts actual scientific findings in order to impose its stereotypical learning machine, together with the risks it poses to autistic people, who are particularly vulnerable to it.

In the psychoanalytic field, following the arguments of Rosine and Robert Lefort, who defined autism as a structure distinct from psychosis, we have seen two different tendencies. Some support the Leforts' thesis and others oppose it, instead claiming that autism should remain part of the psychotic structure. My text will defend the latter hypothesis, while also trying to situate autism topologically.

The biological imaginary

The reason why the theories striving to explain human behaviour on purely biological grounds are thriving is that they produce an illusion, a hope we can find an objective cause and thus minimise subjective responsibility. There is nothing new about this approach: in the early 19th century, anatomists were already trying to establish correlations between the human mind and the shape of the skull. This rather unfruitful pursuit evolved, in the second half of the 19th century, into a search for the links between brain volume and intellectual capacity, only to eventually show, in our time and using medical imaging, the true variability of brain functioning from one individual to another. Far from confirming the supremacy of biology, neurosciences have in fact proven the extent to which language shapes the body:

> While genes and hormones guide the brain development, neural circuitry is essentially constructed through our personal history. If biological

DOI: 10.4324/9781003221487-4

> constraints indeed played a key role in men's and women's behaviour, we would expect to see certain invariants. Yet this is clearly not so.
> (Vidal & Benoit-Browaeys, 2005, p. 92)[2]

MRI studies have shown that performing the same task can activate a number of different areas of the brain, some of them common to all individuals and others radically different. The pattern of the cerebral cortex also varies from one individual to another, including between identical twins.

The modern technologies of "brain imaging" are therefore aptly named: not only because they indeed produce images, but also because they peddle the imaginary. In order to appreciate the strengths but also the limits of magnetic resonance imaging (MRI), we first have to understand its functioning. Its principle is based on the magnetic properties of atoms and molecules, which emit electromagnetic signals when placed in a magnetic field. The computer analysis of these signals enables us to reconstruct images in three-dimensional space. The resulting image is therefore an *interpretation* of data, which is processed based on the knowledge we already have or believe to have. When applied to the brain, this method provides information about brain anatomy and neuronal activity. Anatomical MRI captures the signals of the hydrogen atoms in the water molecules present in the organism; these signals are transmitted depending on their position and environment, allowing us to deduce the nature of the tissues observed. Functional MRI concerns neuronal activity; it does not allow us to measure the electric activity of neurones, but only the influx of oxygenated blood. What is detected is the magnetisation of the haemoglobin molecules, in other words, the volume of blood flow in the given area, rather than the functional state of the neurons. In addition, the time needed to register these signals is usually several minutes, which is a considerable delay compared to the thousandths of a second that it takes for a neuron to fire. The *reconstituted image* is therefore not an image of brain activity in real time, but the product of many hours of processing digital data, which is colour-coded to reconstitute the different areas of the brain. It is not an image of an individual's brain activity, but an interpretation of a certain amount of data. We should therefore be prudent as to the conclusions that we derive from it.

> The fact of having localised the areas of the brain responsible for pain reception does not help us understand the subjective experience of suffering. However, the force of the image is such that we equate "neuronal circuitry" with thought itself. ... a deficit caused by a brain injury shows that the affected area is necessary but not sufficient to perform the given function.
> (ibid., p. 76–77)

To understand the neuroscientific approach, let us take the example described by Gérard Pommier and concerning the region considered to be the brain's pleasure centre: the hypothalamus. In a laboratory, this area of a rat's brain can be stimulated via implanted electrodes, every time the rat pushes a lever.[3] The rats subject to this experiment then cannot stop self-stimulating. The excitation can be blocked in their dopamine receptors by administering pimozide or haloperidol. This type of neurotransmitter blocking is used by psychopharmacology to treat psychosis with drugs similar to haloperidol. However, psychoanalysis did not have to wait for these findings to define the psychoses as a lack of a defence against jouissance, due to the foreclosure of the Name-of-the-father. We could therefore argue that rather than the result of a deficiency in some kind of reward centre of the brain, this excess of jouissance stems from a symbolic failure that the hypothalamus simply records, because the cause of the activation of the neuronal circuitry lies outside rather than inside the organ (like the electrodes in the rat's brain, activated by the lever).

Just like the function produces the organ, the development of neural connections is correlated to their use, which shapes neural synapses. A selective reduction in learning capacity has been observed in animals raised in captivity, who lose the ability to recognise shapes. This reduction in certain capabilities due to non-use is called attrition.

The same phenomenon can be observed in human language acquisition. At birth, a child is able to understand and reproduce an infinite range of sounds, which exceed the phonetic register of his mother tongue. Learning a particular language will therefore leave out a number of sounds and, from a certain age, the child loses his capacity to hear and reproduce them. This observation highlights the way language marks the body, its effects on the living organism. The shaping is not physiological but linguistic. And the language that marks the organism is transmitted by the Other – the sonority of language therefore originates outside the organism itself.

Contrary to animals, who are born with a system of information necessary for their survival, the little human needs to be spoken to, lest the phenomenon of attrition becomes generalised and can even lead to death. The newborn's nervous system is not quite developed; the myelinisation of axons and nerves continues for months after birth, which explains the lack of motor coordination.

This neuronal immaturity is combined with the disproportionate size of the head and the limbs: the human being is born premature. The nervous system is also oversized with regards to the infant's neurological needs, because only one tenth of the neural connections are established at the moment of birth. Finally, pyramidal cells, characterised by clusters of neuron connections needed for information processing, are overabundant and the number of neuron connections continues to increase, both quantitatively and qualitatively, throughout life.

Recent research has shown the extraordinary plasticity of the nervous system. The brain is constantly changing, constantly creating new neuronal circuits based on the stimuli received. There seems to be no innate distribution of the brain regions in early infancy. And even in adulthood, these zones seem to adapt to the circumstances, modifying their connections and showing a high degree of functional interchangeability.

At birth, the new-born's brain includes 100 billion neurons, but only about 10% of the neuron connections or synapses, while 90% of the remaining synapses are constituted over time, reaching the estimated one million billion synapses in adulthood. The 6,000 genes that are involved in the construction of the brain are not enough to control all these synapses. Neuronal development therefore does not depend solely on our genetic makeup. According to Catherine Vidal, in pianists we see a thickening of the areas specialised in finger dexterity, hearing, and vision. In taxi drivers, the regions having to do with spatial representation in the cerebral cortex are highly developed. And we could name other examples that show that brain plasticity remains active, in both directions, progressive and regressive, throughout human life.

Sounds stimulate the neuronal system; via the Other, these sounds acquire a meaning, meaning refers to the sound of another word, which refers to yet another, and so on. To some, this particular place of the Other, responsible for the signifying inscription that grants the subject a body to become embodied in, seems genetically predetermined. Has "the preformationist interpretation of molecular genetics ... been successful because it responds to a magical need for explanation?" (Pommier, 2004, p. 62).

"In order to look and to hear, we need to define the position from which to look, from which to hear, define it symbolically" (Vanier, 1993, p. 39). The mirror stage, concomitant with the jubilatory assumption of an "I", conditions the construction of the body and the unification of its image via nomination, which is transmitted to the subject by the person holding him. Without this nomination, which creates a gap between the mirror image and the living body, "the specular image becomes the image of the double, with all the radical uncanniness it brings" (Lacan, 2016, p. 47). If the gaze does not establish this structuring gap of the mirror stage via the Other's naming of the subject, there will be no identification and the child will either remain "stuck" to the image or try and imitate it. The Other and the fellow human being can then only exist in this logic of the double. Lacan writes: "In relation to what it duplicates, the specular image is exactly the right glove becoming the left glove, which one can obtain on a single surface by turning the rim inside out" (ibid., p. 96).

This turning inside out cannot happen on a one-sided surface, because the lack of distinction between the "front" and the "back" of the Mobius strip or the cross-cap makes the surface non-specularisable. This corresponds to the autist's topology, where the signifying marking did not produce a cut and there is no access to the mirror stage.

Standing in front of the mirror, Donna Williams[4] therefore sees, at a particular moment, something that reminds her of a piece of rubbish, with all the anxiety and horror such image can provoke. Then she sees her double, Carol, in the image of herself reflected in the mirror. Unable to recognise herself, she instead believes she is looking at another person. She throws herself against the mirror to try and get through into Carol's world. The double manifests something of herself, something of the object *a*, while also giving it a frame.

Biological autism

The first babbling of the child, immerged in the glottic jouissance that contains an endless variety of sounds, will gradually be filled by the musicality of the Other (the mother or her substitute), through which something of the order of enunciation will mark the birth of the subject, what Lacan calls *lalangue*. The baby is "entirely absorbed in the hearing of his voice and his phonematic signifier, which Lacan described as the unary signifier, the S_1" (Lefort & Lefort, 1997). This coupling between the object-voice (the object *a*) and S_1 spells the subject's entry into speech, an entry confirmed by the Other, to whom the child is speaking and who responds by giving meaning to the child's enjoyment of these vocalisations, shaped by the musicality of the mother tongue. When recognised as a subject, the child accepts the meaning given by the Other to the sounds he is producing and in this way appropriates the Other's language, making it his own. The subject is then inscribed in the gap between S_1 and S_2, where the S_2, that produces meaning also puts a stop to jouissance, marking a shift towards *j'ouïs-sens* ("I hear meaning") and also *jouis-sens* ("enjoy-meant"). This S_2 established by the Other is the expression of the Other's desire; hence the Other is de-completed. The metonymy of *essaim* ("swarm"), the S_1, the signifier, comes to a halt in the metaphor of S_1/S_2, anticipating the paternal metaphor, in which the Symbolic is established as a hole. In his "Geneva lecture on the symptom", Lacan says that in the autist, like in the schizophrenic, "there is something ... which freezes" (Lacan, 1989, p. 20), referring to his previous theorisation of the "solidification" of the signifying pair S_1-S_2 (Lacan, 1998, p. 235). In the absence of symbolisation, words take on a specific meaning for the autist, plunging them into an endless repetition. He uses them as reality indicators in an unchangeable world. This is why autists are so interested in lists: directories, train timetables, calendars, road signs and so on, in other words, ordered sets of signifiers isolated from one another, contrary to the relationships established between the elements of a novel or a text. The function of the letter is dominant, because it refers to a fragmented world. People with autism often have significant capacities of remembering and recall, and they are able to carry out complex calculations. For Freud, remembering is the absence of repression. If there is no repression, there is no return of the repressed and things seem simply "there", unconnected, or rather only connected momentarily, because the temporal dimension seems to have been abolished. This ordered, non-barred Other makes it possible to localise jouissance by delimiting certain fields. Such mechanisation of the Other can have calming effects, even though the process of separation has not taken place.

However, we seem to observe the same phenomenon among the advocates of a purely biological model, who also tend to reduce life to a mechanical programme. The language of the genome then becomes binary, just like computer language. In order to counterbalance this mechanical vision of the living organism, certain scientists introduced, in the 1990s, the so-called epigenetic paradigm: the organism interacts with its environment, which enables and affects gene expression. In this perspective, our genetic potential is dependent on non-innate agents, which are part of the organism itself or a relationship that affects it. However, people do not just adapt to their environment, they also transform it. And this transformation is only possible thanks to the inscription of the symbolic. Culture, as Lévi-Strauss argued, has become man's natural milieu. In the middle ages, Frederic II of Sicily conducted an experiment to show that Latin was a natural language: he had a group of children raised in isolation, without any speech being addressed to them. Of course, none of the children survived. Outside the scientific discourse, which operates "by imagining the real of the symbolic" (Lacan, Seminar of 13th November 1973), autism and the ideology of biological determinism share the same topological structure: by rejecting the hole of the Symbolic, this ideology remains trapped in the very psychosis it is claiming to explain. We could argue that it is not autism that is biological, but the ideology of biological determinism that is autistic.

Body and language

If the Other fails to give meaning to the child's cry, the cry cannot become a call. Meaning and signification cannot operate; the cry remains simply a physiological excitation. Among the autistic people described by Kanner as "deaf", because they seem indifferent to human voice, we can observe a silent movement of the lips. Sometimes they appear to be following orders others cannot hear. Lacan says that "autists hear themselves" just like everyone else (Lacan, 1989, p. 19). The phenomenon of speech means that we can hear the sound of our own words. The emitting subject is at the same time the receiving subject, but as the emitter he has received his message from the Other. There is thus, at the same time, the relationship of the subject to the Other's discourse and to his own speech. These relationships differ in neurosis and in psychosis. The crucial question is to know where we hear ourselves from. In psychosis, the subject receives his message directly from the real Other, who is also the emitter. In the phenomenon of psycho-motor verbal hallucinations, we see the outlines of phonatory movements – the subject himself articulates what he hears as spoken by his voices. Hearing in this sense can concern the signifying chain or the sound modulation of speech. Like Schreber, who feels obliged to complete the interrupted sentences he hears, the autistic child, having rejected words, can only recreate sounds without meaning: "Not all autists hear voices, but they articulate lots of things, and what they articulate, it is a matter of discovering where they heard it" (ibid.). For Lacan, autists are "rather verbose" (p. 20), from the Latin *verbosus, verbum*, meaning speech. The word "verbose" means using too many words to say something: too much speech and too few ideas. If the word tries to pin down the thing, the verbose person is someone whose words remain unmoored from things. Lacan therefore highlights the loss of the semantic value of words and consequently the loss of their enjoyable resonance, because no presence, of either the subject or the Other, resonates in what is being said. The autist seems to refuse becoming alienated in the Other's language. Muteness, insofar as it means not giving in to the jouissance of the object-voice, is the most radical form of this refusal. When the subject does speak, the language is not inhabited, without affect; the voice seems artificial and inexpressive. Echolalia, a jerky or monotonous tone, can be seen as the signs of the absence of a position of enunciation. Hence it is easier for autists to learn language via writing or online, where the jouissance of the voice is excluded.

In many clinical descriptions, starting with Leo Kanner's princeps case (1943, p. 217–230), the bodies of autistic children appear disaffected. There is something mechanical, nearly robotic, about their way of walking: often they tip-toe and lean forward, as if trying not to fall. They may perform repetitive movements and sometimes harm themselves severely. In general, they have good manual dexterity when engaged in solitary activities and do not tolerate well when someone tries to show them another way of doing things. They seem to be looking out into the space and avoiding the gaze of others; sometimes their gaze appears empty and the subject absent, as if in a stupor. We may wonder if they can hear us when we speak to them. If they can enter into contact with us, it is usually fleetingly and temporarily, for example not responding when they are called. Their bodies function as armour, a "fortress" in which the child is locked and which shelters him from any contact with others. They often have little sensitivity to warmth or cold, and even to pain, but their internal organs function correctly, and these children are generally in good physical health. Everything happens as if the only affected functions were those that mark the body in a signifying way, mediated by the Other. In some cases, we observe that organic functions acquired early on as reflexes are lost during therapy: in many cases it is toilet training, because defecating is the main activity through which the Other's demand is introduced. The act of defecation, which brings being together, is the constitution of the subject as one. For the autist, the impossibility of separation prevents the excrement from becoming an object he can let go of and which could intervene in his relationship to the Other. Organic activities therefore function for as long as they escape the Other's demand, while the gaze and the voice, which are correlated to the Other's desire, remain problematic. The autist's relationship to his own body is therefore marked by the lack of inscription of the signifier: "The first body [the symbolic body] makes the second [the 'naïve' body] by embodying itself in it" (Lacan, 2001, p. 409).

Bernard Nominé (2012) relates the autist's position to Hegel's position of the slave, of whom Lacan says that what unites the master and the slave in a discourse is the slave's body having become the metaphor of the master's jouissance. This position of the slave is only made possible by the slave not confounding himself with what his body represents for the master. His own object *a*, the object of jouissance, remains outside the framework of what alienates him and separates him from the master. For the autist, the body has not been pierced through by the falling away of the object *a*, a falling away that also makes a hole in the Other. Because of this lack of the hole produced by the signifying cut, the subject can embody the object of the Other's jouissance:

> If the Other has not lost anything, the real object remains included in him; the subject misses the signifier of his Ⱥ and confronts the real object he includes in himself, as well as his Other, by embodying the Other's real object.
> (Lefort & Lefort, 1988, p. 597)

Remaining inside the autistic "bubble" is a precarious means of defence against being swallowed up, annihilated by the Other, and thus falling into an abyss of anxiety.

The autist can find another solution in a coupling with a supplementary eroticised object, an object of jouissance outside the body, which belongs to the category of objects *a* and which the subject's body can either become "stuck" to or that can be held at a distance and rejected.

The object *a* is constituted via the outside:

> the mamma is in some way stuck on, implanted on the mother. This is what allows it to function structurally at the level of the *a*, which is defined as something from which the child is separated in a way that is internal to the sphere of his existence.
> (Lacan, 2016, p. 234)

For the autist, the object remains stuck to the child and it is only its metonymic substitute that helps him come alive, a kind of double he can control and manipulate, that he can use to "stick to" the Other. The object establishes a border between the subject and the Other.

"As surrounding circles or border lines, [patterns] were set up as a means of protection from invasion from that which exists outside, in 'the world'" (Williams, 2009, p. 185). The borders the autistic subject constructs using the object as a double and/or an imaginary or hallucinated double provide protection from the external world perceived as hostile. This border can then help him develop significant abilities, including becoming highly erudite in one or several well-defined fields. Containing jouissance within these limits can sometimes make it possible to have a professional life.

The question of the object, concrete or hallucinated, which is used to create a border against a jouissance that would otherwise annihilate the subject in the Other, is very present in Donna Williams' work: "There was something overwhelming that always seemed too powerful in giving in to physical touch. It was the threat of losing all sense of separateness between myself and the other person. Like being eaten up" (ibid., p. 117). Without the consistent limitation of her double (Carol), Donna no longer has a body: "I ... began to hurt myself in order to feel something" (p. 56). The hallucinated other and/or the concrete object that embodies the other produces a kind of localisation of jouissance. Williams continues: "For me, the people I liked *were* their things, and those things (or things like them) were the protection from the things I didn't like – other people. ... Communication via objects was safe" (p. 13–14).

Structure and the autistic "making do"

Rosine and Robert Lefort drew up a list of differences between autism and schizophrenia. Autistic people do not suffer from delusions. The time of the appearance of the earliest manifestations differs. According to the Leforts, "there is no Other and therefore no object, because the subject would not know how to make the Other carry the object". For these authors, the absence of the Other and the object constitutes a fundamental difference between autism and psychosis. However, the fact that the Other is not present as complete, without the signifying cut that traces the outlines of the objects *a*, does not necessarily mean that there is no Other at all. Rather we could say that there is no barred Other. The autistic person is outside discourse but not outside language. Child autism is not muteness. Autistic children are in language and only a small minority do not speak at all or only very little. Most of them have a particular relationship to language, which is of the order of repetition, not in the Freudian sense but as a kind of automatic language that can, but does not have to, include echolalia. Also, their different relationship to the Other is not the manifestation of a specific structure, but rather the consequences of a different form of the foreclosure of the Name-of-the-father. Despite their claims about the absence of the Other and the object, the Leforts nevertheless speak about the drive in autism, even though they see it as reduced to only the death drive: "the death drive operates against the subject, producing masochistic jouissance" (Lefort & Lefort, 2003, p. 53).

If the drive is the echo of the signifier in the body, we could say that in the autist's body the signifier resonates in its function of the death of the thing. The autist seems persecuted by the signs of the Other's presence, especially those linked to two forms of the object *a*, the gaze and the voice. The question is then not so much of conceptualising a structure distinct from psychosis, but of distinguishing between two ways of handling jouissance when faced with the foreclosure of the Name-of-the-father.

Following the Leforts' thesis, which posits the existence of an autistic structure distinct from psychosis, Jean-Claude Maleval, who defines autism on the basis of the foreclosure of the Name-of-the-father, establishes a series of distinctions between the two structures and especially between autism and schizophrenia. He identifies two main differences:

1   The border or edge (*le bord*), which he defines as a boundary constructed by the autistic subject in order to isolate his world from the world of others. As long as he stays within the surface delimited by these boundaries, he feels safe. Maleval makes this border a specificity of autism and a point of distinction from schizophrenia: "Children who have not constructed the specifically autistic defence, which is supported by a border, or whose defences have been crushed by having the object taken away from them, are indeed very difficult to distinguish from schizophrenics" (Maleval, 2010).
2   Another difference concerns language in autism:

> there is no retention of the voice in schizophrenia or paranoia; there is no compensation by a "sign language" (in schizophrenia, we can see this from time to time, but it is rather exceptional). We might also see a particular object being given a privileged position by the schizophrenic, but this too is fairly exceptional … For the schizophrenic, the unary signifier has been set up, i.e., jouissance is ciphered by the signifier.
>
> (ibid.)

However, while the autistic subject struggles to cipher jouissance by the unary signifier, he does manage to establish a functional language, disconnected from jouissance, while maintaining

> another language that is caught up in the signifier and with this language connected to jouissance the subject is quite verbose, he speaks to himself. … There is an S_1 in the verbose language, but not in the functional language.
>
> (ibid.)

The S_1 is there, but it is protected by the autistic "bubble" and thus hidden away from the Other's gaze and hearing.

It seems to me that these points of distinction do not constitute a separate structure, but a way of "making do" with the foreclosure of the Name-of-the-father, in order to maintain some articulation between the different registers and allowing the subject to live in the world. This is akin to the hysterical and obsessional modalities of neurosis, which too show us two different ways of "making do" with the Name-of-the-father as a sinthome. Neither in neurosis nor in psychosis do we see these modalities in their pure form. Hence the importance of understanding the way in which the real, symbolic and imaginary are tied together for a concrete subject: "Jouissance is very precisely correlated with the initial form of the entry into play of what I am calling the mark" (Lacan, 2008, p. 177/206).

All happens as if the autistic rigidity was a way of maintaining of a pseudo-Borromean link, as Lacan presents it in Seminar XXIII *The Sinthome*, where the failure in the primitive knotting can produce a kind of folding that resembles a knot with three rings, but nevertheless can be unfolded into a single ring that only encloses a void:

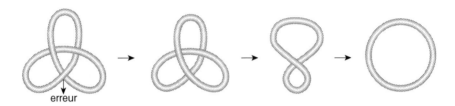

Figure 3.1

The only possible remedy is to construct an extra "buckle", the loop of the sinthome, which will "lock" the trefoil knot, preventing it from coming loose:

Figure 3.2

For the autist, this buckle of the sinthome has not been produced and the subject remains frozen in a fragile folding that can come undone at any moment. The rigidity and anticipation of situations help maintain the structure in place. Anything that disrupts this precarious equilibrium can undo the folding and cast the subject into an infinite abyss of jouissance, into a state of perplexity or stupor, from which he can only emerge by screaming or via a passage-to-the-act. The latter can take the form of destructive violence against objects or other people, but also against oneself, through self-harming or seizures.

The smallest change is immediately detected and often results in an absolute need to return to the previous state; not even the least metonymic sliding is bearable. This is very clearly perceived by Temple Grandin, who writes that some autists are "incapable of making simple generalisations" (Grandin, 2006, p. 185). For her, the "rigid behaviour and inability to generalize may be partly due to having little or no ability to change or modify visual memories" (p. 22). "Such people are not able to comprehend any deviations from the pictures in their memory" (p. 186).

The deficiency in the primitive knotting, which leaves the autistic subject's "knot" a mere folding resembling a trefoil, can find a stabilising solution if a suppletion can be produced to hold the folding in place, in the form of a double. The function of the double, which we find in Grandin's text in several forms, seems to have led her to reach a certain stability, holding the folded loop together. It also propelled her towards her chosen career, after an encounter with a "squeeze chute" at her aunt's ranch. A "squeeze chute" is a handling facility that immobilises cattle during delousing, vaccination, or castration. The animal's panic disappeared when it was tightly held in the machine. Grandin's gaze was captivated by this experience and she decided to experiment on herself: "for me, [the chute] served two functions: First, it provided stimulation ... and containment, which helped me relax; secondly, it provided a warm, soft, comfortable environment, which helped me receive and give affection" (Grandin & Scariano, 1996, p. 125). This is not an identification. There is no metaphorical or metonymic function; instead the subject is stuck to, submerged in the other's image.

> When I put myself in a cow's place, I really have to be that cow and not a person in a cow costume. I use my visual thinking skills to simulate what an animal would see and hear in a given situation. I place myself inside its body and imagine what it experiences. ... I also have to imagine what experiencing the world through the cow's sensory system is like.
> (Grandin, 2006, p. 168)

This experience conveys "what is involved when *a* enters the world of the real, to which in fact it is simply returning" (Lacan, 2016, p. 99).

Temple dreamt of inventing another kind of magic machine. This obsessive fixation, as she herself defines it, led her to study "animal science" and later to a career in a related field: she became one of the few global experts in cattle handling equipment. The chute became "the squeeze machine", of which Grandin went on to construct a series of models.[5]

We could wonder whether what Grandin is "squeezing" in her machine, via the cow as a double, is not her own subjective consistency, maintaining the folding resembling the knot that constitutes her as a subject, while at the same time letting her affix her proper name to her function as a "cattle handling expert", thus limiting her jouissance. For Leo Kanner, a certain stabilisation was possible to obtain if the autist developed his fixation into a professional career.

Maleval distinguishes between three elements that can help create a boundary to the autistic jouissance: the double, the object (the autistic object) and an area of competence (Maleval, 2010). These three elements often appear interwoven and non-differentiable. However, they can also acquire a degree of differentiation, just like in the case of Grandin: the cow that occupies the position of the double can be contained through the object, the dip vat, which is developed and improved thanks to her knowledge in the field and which leads her to embrace the career of a "cattle management specialist" and in turn maintain a certain fixation of her jouissance. It is as if this discovery helped her stabilise these three elements – which can be associated with the three registers constituting the subject – making the initial folding induced by the foreclosure of the Name-of-the-father "stick". I do not think this is a case of a nomination via the "buckle" of the sinthome, which would require the subject to make a hole in the enjoying substance of the living being, but rather the result of gluing the rings of the knot to a single surface and the subject remains submerged in the space of the non-barred Other. Immersion is different from embedding, due to the lack of distinction between the over and under movements of the strings.

The space inhabited by the autist is a frozen two-dimensional space, which has lost the mobility generated by the embedding of the circles in three-dimensional space. While it prevents the knot from coming undone and leaving the subject faced with the engulfing void of infinite jouissance, once it has been found this solution can also help him develop a creative and social activity, and thus a degree of integration in the world of others.

The challenge of autism

If the signifying cut cannot be inscribed, not only does the body of the subject remain without a hole, but neither is any object removed from the Other's body. The Other is seen in his entirety as an object. Because the Other does

Figure 3.3 Embedding

Figure 3.4 Immersion

not have any "holes" created by the Symbolic, the circuit of the drive, insofar as it is the signifier resonating in the body, cannot be properly established. The living being remains submerged in a real of pure and undifferentiated jouissance. The consistency of the symbolic Other depends on his incompleteness. If the Other's object-voice cannot be perceived as an object the Other can cede, the Other's speech cannot fulfil its role in transmission and instead becomes intrusive.

This is why the forcible use of various educational methods can only be experienced as an intrusion from the Other who, by violating the defensive armour protecting the subject, triggers panic and anxiety. Because of the violence involved, these so-called educational approaches indeed can be seen as a form of abuse. The advocates of the (behaviourist) ABA method or the (cognitivist) TEACCH programme seem to know nothing about the elementary features of the autistic pathology and instead reduce the subject to a trainable animal; their theories of autism too are deduced from biological research conducted on animals.

Following their perspective and given the diversity of behaviours observed among autistic patients, it was imperative to explore the entire brain. Because the findings did not appear to incriminate a particular region of the brain, scientists had to look at the different groups of neurones. When they did not find any explanation for the simultaneous dysfunction of several neuronal groups, they invented the concept of *minimal brain damage*. This only confirms Godel's famous theorem, i.e. that any system can either be inconsistent or incomplete. Once biology begins to look for completeness, it can only turn out to be inconsistent. The same is true for cognitivism, originating in the code-breaking research of World War II. The artificial intelligence research derived from these efforts has equated neural circuitry with digital circuitry. By adhering to a connectionist theory of psychic functioning, cognitivism has reduced the subject to simply one element in the system.

The ABA method, founded by Ole Ivar Lovaas, is a coercive learning method, which consists in repeatedly presenting the child with a stimulus and, depending on his response, introducing either a reward or a punishment, such as the electroshocks initially used by Lovaas, now supposedly abandoned. The coercive aspect of the method also lies in its application to children who perceive any demand as intrusive and threatening, and who, suffice to say, are not asked for their consent. However, the so-called "high-functioning" autists have shown the importance of being given a space in which they can find their own solutions to their anxiety and create social relationships. Annick Deshays speaks about an approach to autism which considers the person's singularity and refuses all kinds of preestablished teaching programmes: "Using the behaviourist approach means trying to make us more 'pliable' through a kind of formatting that reduces our freedom of expression. It means deepening our already serious problems of identification and humanisation" (Deshays, 2009,

p. 120–121). She adds: "thinking instead of us means running the risk of abolishing the very essence of our reason for existence" (p. 124).

The educational forcing of ABA and TEACH, based on repetitive and stereotyped learning (of the same content in regular and fixed sequences), reduces the subject to simply an object and can therefore only deepen the autistic isolation. One form of defence against the anxiety of being submerged in the Other's jouissance is precisely to adopt, by simple imitation, the expected behaviour, without actually being able to appropriate it: "Instead of talking with people, I would merely mimic them" (Williams, 2009, p. 26). "The sensing of a ghost watching me as I allowed people to play on my characters to which I'd respond accordingly ... as an actress in my body, in a state of automation" (ibid., p. 124). For learning to happen, each autistic subject has to find his own way; in order to do this, they can often use the double or the autistic object placed in its position. This means that we must let their own self-knowledge emerge, a singular knowledge that runs contrary to the ideology of reducing differences and globalising behaviours. Or are these methods in fact trying to better integrate autists in the capitalist mode of production and consumption?

> Just like the invention of the intelligence quotient helped homogenize the individual vis-à-vis a certain conception of knowledge as a way of capitalising on knowledges (units of value), the theory of addiction claims that the individual only wants what the market supplies. In all cases the subject is conflated with the individual, in order words, made complete via a surplus-enjoyment "kit".
>
> (Sauret & Alberti, 1997, p. 120)

In this way, both neurosciences and cognitivism respond to the political imperative of profitability as the key principle of mental health policies.

> The development of neurosciences opens up new and important economic perspectives. In the United States, the psychotropic drugs market, the "neurocomputing" market ... and even the market of "brain games" designed to "strengthen your synapses" are booming.
>
> (Vidal & Benoit-Browaeys, 2005, p. 83)

At the same time, biologists themselves have protested, based on the paradoxical results of their research, against the supposedly strictly biological origin of autism and have argued that other, non-biological determinants must also be found. Blind to the ex-sistence of the subject, they are looking for these not in language but in the environment, in other words, in the maternal organism. However, although the contingencies of this organism of course do affect the subject's relationship to the Other, it is the symbolic that produces the Other's body to become embodied in. "The biological reality of existence is superimposed onto the pre-existing signifying chain, where the place of the subject, like any object, is signified through a name" (Aulagnier, 1965).

Notes

1 This text was originally published in *Champ lacanien*, 15 (2014/1): 151–171.
2 Catherine Vidal is a neurobiologist, Director of Research at the Institute Pasteur.
3 This so-called "brain stimulation reward" experiment was first carried out by James Olds and Peter Milner in 1954 and reported in *Science* 127, p. 315–324. For a discussion see Pommier, 2004, p. 15.
4 Australian multidisciplinary artist (painter, writer, sculptor, musician), born in Melbourne, Victoria, in 1963.
5 Her technique of containing and calming the subject in fact resembles the controversial method of "packing".

References

Aulagnier, P. (1965). Presentation on 28 April 1965. In Lacan, J., *Séminaire, livre XII: Les problèmes cruciaux de la psychanalyse*. Unpublished.
Deshays, A. (2009). *Libres propos philosophiques d'une autiste*. Paris: Presses de la Renaissance.
Grandin, T. (2006). *Thinking in Pictures: And Other Reports from My Life with Autism*. London: Bloomsbury.
Grandin, T. & Scariano, M. (1996). *Emergence: Labelled Autistic*. New York: Warner Books Press.
Kanner, L. (1943). Autistic disturbances of affective contact. *Nervous Child*, 2, 217–250. Reprinted in: *Acta Paedo-Psychiatrica*, 35(4), 100–136.
Lacan, J. (1974). *Séminaire, livre XXI: Les non-dupes errent*. Unpublished.
Lacan, J. (1989). Geneva lecture on the symptom (1975). *Analysis*, 1, 7–26.
Lacan, J. (1998). *The Seminar, Book XI: The Four Fundamental Concepts of Psychoanalysis*. New York: Norton.
Lacan, J. (2001). Radiophonie. *Autres écrits*. Paris: Seuil.
Lacan J. (2008). *Seminar, Book XII: The Other Side of Psychoanalysis*. New York: Norton.
Lacan, J. (2016). *Seminar, Book X: Anxiety*. Cambridge: Polity Press.
Lefort, R. & Lefort, R. (1988). *Les structures de la psychose*. Paris: Seuil.
Lefort, R. & Lefort, R. (2003). *La distinction de l'autisme*. Paris: Seuil.
Lefort, R. & Lefort, R. (1997). L'accès de l'enfant à la parole condition du lien social. *Bulletin du Groupe Petite Enfance*, 10.
Maleval, J-C. (2010). *Qui sont les autistes? Lecture for the Association Le Pont Freudien*, 19 February 2010 in Montreal.
Nominé, B. (2012). *L'enfant autiste et son corps. Une approche psychomotrice de l'autisme infantile*. Paris: Editions in press.
Pommier, G. (2004). *Comment les sciences démontrent la Psychanalyse*. Paris: Flammarion.
Sauret, M-J. & Alberti, C. (1997). L'intérêt de l'autisme. *Bulletin du Groupe Petite Enfance*, 10.

Vanier, A. (1993). Autisme, théorie et position de l'analyste. In *Hommage à Frances Tustin*. Saint-André- de-Cruzières: Audit.
Vidal, C. & Benoit-Browaeys, D. (2005). *Cerveau Sexe & Pouvoir*. Paris: Belin.
Williams, D. (2009). *Nobody Nowhere: The Remarkable Autobiography of an Autistic Girl*. London: Jessica Kingsley Publishers.

Chapter 4

Autists, practitioners, and institutions
The abuse of reductionism[1]

Jean-Pierre Drapier

It has been difficult to ignore, and not only in France, the controversies, disputes, discussions, questions, and hypotheses concerning autism, its aetiology as well as the appropriate care and treatment.

These questions are being posed by all sides and yet seem unresolvable. But let's just remember the famous Columbus egg, a problem impossible to solve without first reframing the question, namely breaking off the tip of the egg – a simple yet robust solution. Just as simple as cutting the Gordian knot.

And so, to resolve the question of autism, let's begin with a simple idea, but one that comes the closest to the real: "Autism does not exist". In other words, let's start by smashing the object of the controversy. It is a well-established epistemological fact that a poorly identified problem or an ill-defined topic of inquiry can cause the imagination to run wild, so that all kinds of arguments become acceptable, depending on one's point of view. Some psychiatrists and psychoanalysts thus wrongly reduced the question of autism to its psychogenetic aspects, promoting a kind of monism of both aetiology and form.

Not all of them fell into this trap, of course: neither Frances Tustin (1992), who at the end of her life preferred to speak about "autistic states", nor Margaret Mahler (1979), who wrote about the "autistic syndrome" and saw autism as one pole of a continuum.

Today, certain scientists are committing the same methodological error, when they adopt a scientific approach that reduces all autistic syndromes to the so-called "neurodevelopmental autism" with allegedly purely organic causes, thus rendering any subjective angle completely irrelevant. This methodological reasoning is equally misguided: why would the existence of an organic cause do away with subjective suffering and make it useless for the subject to try to elaborate his own world? The existence of the symbolic order, the order of language, concerns all of us, including those who reject it.

So, you might ask, are you rejecting this diagnosis completely, shying away from it and potentially delaying a treatment that should be offered as early as

DOI: 10.4324/9781003221487-5

possible? Not at all! I fully agree with Jean Oury: "Diagnosis is a serious matter". It is serious, because it has consequences, especially for the therapeutic strategy and the analyst's position, but also for the transference, interpretation, and the style of interventions, for the combination of different treatments and so on. It is precisely because it is a serious matter that we should take it seriously, instead of being swayed by the fashionable or dominant discourses endorsed by the media and politicians. As of now, there are only four diagnostic categories for children with mental difficulties in France: they are either "gifted", suffer from "learning difficulties", are "hyperactive", or "autistic". In nine out of ten cases this is a false diagnosis concealing a real one, which we could call anxiety, neurosis, psychosis, autistic disorders, the cause of which has to be identified. The problem with these stereotypical diagnoses is that they lead to stereotypical treatments and the denial of the child's subjectivity: just give him some medication, re-educate him, and all will be well.

The clinic shows that this is not so: the patient's suffering and difficulties continue. Even though the zealots of these neo-diagnoses often believe they are critiquing the psychiatric approach, they remain confined by its diagnostic method, which favours observable phenomena and aims to establish a series in a collection of elements: such and such sign corresponds to such and such diagnosis, which corresponds to such and such treatment. The treatments are standardised, stereotypical, dictated by the computer. An autistic child I had treated for a number of years returned for his second "evaluation" to a CRA[2] in Paris. The results of this otherwise rigorous assessment pointed out the significant progress made by the child in terms of his behaviour, relationships, speech, absence of delusions and hallucinations, and consistent schooling. Conclusion: "Continue treatment at the CMPP.[3] Also implement ABA therapy and Risperdal 1mg." One diagnosis, one treatment. In this case, although the diagnosis was correct (even though it said "autism" instead of "autistic syndrome"), the automatic and universalising response (all children with autism must receive ABA and Risperidone) constitutes a real danger.

The present-day scientific discourse has created an enormous sack labelled "Autism", where it puts anything that seems to show the same signs; it then concludes that all these conditions have the same neurodevelopmental origin and therefore require the same treatment.

However, in a properly constructed nosography this kind of clustering does not constitute a nosographic entity, i.e. an illness, but only a syndrome, a set of symptoms. Let's look at the example of the depressive syndrome. It is defined by its symptomatic traits (aboulia or the loss of desire, sadness, crying, sleep disturbances) and its psychical mechanisms (loss of drive, avoidance of things that are difficult to tolerate, and so on). At one point, some wanted to transform it into a nosographic entity, "depressive illness". This did not work very well, because who would confuse a reactive depression with mourning, a neurotic position with melancholia? Today, this large sack called autism presents us with the same methodological trick.

Let's go back to the basics. At different ages, parents tell us, a child begins to show relational or communicational difficulties. They say this very clearly: "When he was born, he wouldn't look at us. Holding him was like holding a piece of wood." Or, on the contrary: "When he was nine months old, he stopped developing, he regressed, he would only eat in this or that way." Others say: "When he was 16 months old, he was able to say: 'papa, mama, popo', he was walking, but since then nothing more has happened, and he has become aggressive."

Already the fact that these things occur at very different developmental stages should put a question mark over the idea of etiological unicity. Moreover, the screenings, which are becoming more systematic (and rightly so!), show that only in 20% of cases is an organic factor found: a fragile X chromosome, a deleted gene, Trisomy 4p (a few cases in literature), Rett syndrome, etc. In 80% of cases nothing is found, no doubt in part because of our lack of knowledge, but also because there is nothing organic to be found. Why systematically deny the existence of accidents and unfortunate encounters in the subject's history? Also, why not think that these "environmental" causes, which include the child's historicised signifying coordinates, may fall on more or less "receptive" ground? Psychic causality and organic causality are not necessarily incompatible.

In any event, the highly heterogenous nature of its appearance, aetiology, and development is what has led me to reject the notion of "autism" as a unified diagnostic entity and instead speak of "autistic syndrome", which I define as follows:

- Persecution by the Other and the signs of his existence: the gaze, voice, touch, desire, will, orders, superego injunctions, changes in one's surroundings. All these signs mark the presence of the Other, his existence in the *Umwelt*, and his radical difference from the subject's fragile *Innenwelt*. The Other is intrusive and dangerous.
- This persecution and danger are responded to by trying to abolish the Other: through silence or idiosyncratic language, by refusing to look or touch, through the need for immutability, the need to nullify the presence and desire of the one or several little others, through the autist's superb form of ignorance, through aggressiveness, or by reducing the other to a utilitarian extension.
- The non-construction of an imaginarised body structured by the signifier, especially the limbs and body orifices, which leads to eating disorders, poor continence management, problems with walking, and so on.

In other words, there is a set of symptoms and attitudes towards the world that enables us to speak about "autists", in the same way we speak about the depressed or alcoholics, but avoiding the confusing categories of autism, depressive illness, or alcoholism. The formal envelope of the symptom can obscure structural differences, leading to vague diagnoses and thus to uniformised and faulty therapeutic decisions.

Given its fundamental methodological flaws, this reductionist approach can only be imposed by force, while disregarding logic or reason. Hence the abusive practices we *support* regarding autists, institutions, and practitioners alike. Where there is no logical authority, only authoritarian arguments remain.

These approximative diagnoses, the inclusion criteria of which are continuously expanding, also have another consequence: alongside the false ADHD epidemic, they have led to the creation of a false autism epidemic, a form of statistical expansionism.

In the United States, the prevalence of ADHD among children aged six to 17 increased from 0.7% in 1996 to 2% in 2001, and then to 5.3% in 2007. Meanwhile, in the UK the number is 1.16% and in France between 0.01% (Institut Pasteur) and 0.064% (the French National Authority for Health; the Fombonne study, 2009). Together with other criteria (autism and not PDD), this figure would increase from four per 10,000 in 1966–1976 to 20 per 10,000 after 2000.

This etiological and methodological reductionism leads to statistical expansionism, an authoritarian attitude (all think as one), and therefore to the abuse (in all senses of the term) of autists, clinicians, and institutions, both theoretically and practically.

What is the solution? First of all, pluralism. I do not wish to promote psychoanalysis as the only approach to treating autists, nor as the only tool for understanding their mysterious world. At the same time, I believe that because its method is based on structure and dynamics rather than on the formal envelope of the symptom, psychoanalysis can greatly aid diagnosis and ensure that we avoid putting everything in the same bag.

This means we have to make a slightly longer detour and look at the question of psychoanalytic – specifically Lacanian – diagnosis from two different but not necessarily incompatible vantage points: one based on the unconscious-as-language, the other on the real, Borromean unconscious.

The unconscious-as-language and structure

"The signifier represents the subject for another signifier" – we are all familiar with this Lacanian maxim. Let's make it our starting point and examine it by following the processes of alienation and separation. First, we have the human organism, which comes into the world helpless and crying (S). His first step towards becoming human will be being named, placed under the signifier S1, or rather several signifiers, the "swarm" (*essaim*) of S1. This is written as:

$$\uparrow \frac{S_1}{S}$$

Figure 4.1

This is the process of signifying alienation, the alienation of having to be represented by signifiers. The autist remains on the edge of this alienation, unaffected by it, or not yet affected, if we assume that for some children autism is not a definitive structure. In any case, the only structure that could really claim to be autistic is this kind of wavering of the signifying alienation, while remaining a pure S.

The psychotic never moves beyond this point: he remains alienated in the signifier, petrified under a signifier S_1, a *solidified* signifier that no longer refers to another signifier. In this sense, the psychotic is in language – we could even say that he suffers from it (*il en pâtit*), in the sense of passion, but because this S_1 is not articulated to any S_2, he remains outside discourse. Neither autists nor psychotics are outside language. On the contrary: they are very sensitive to it and the effects of signifiers on them are sometimes remarkable, and not always in the pacifying sense! Then we have another process, which is that of a separation by the signifier:

$$\uparrow \frac{S_1 \rightarrow S_2}{S}$$

Figure 4.2

The subject falls under S_1, but the S_1 is included in the signifying chain by its articulation to S_2, where the S_1 then represents the subject for another signifier. This has three consequences:

- First, a mortification, a loss of jouissance, the production of what Lacan called the "object that falls away", the object *a*.

$$\frac{S_1}{S} \rightarrow \frac{S_2}{a} \downarrow$$

Figure 4.3

- Then, because of this separation, of this division by "his" S_1 and the loss of jouissance, the subject is divided, split, barred.

$$\frac{S_1}{\$} \to \frac{S_2}{a} \downarrow$$

Figure 4.4

- Finally (I say *first, then, finally* purely for convenience, we should think of these moments synchronically rather than diachronically), the neurotic is radically separated from his object *a*. He has no direct access to his jouissance and must go through the circuit of the signifying chain.

$$\uparrow \frac{S_1}{\$} \to \frac{S_2}{//\ a} \downarrow$$

Figure 4.5

This is the matheme of the unconscious, or, if you wish, the structure that represents the neurotic.

We should also notice that the discourse of the unconscious is in every respect homogeneous with the discourse of the master. This is Lacan's description of the Freudian unconscious, with the idea that the subject's truth is ultimately represented by his symptom, in S_1, and that this S_1 is articulated to the unconscious knowledge through the elaboration, in the treatment, of multiple S_2. These S_2 give a meaning to the neurotic's symptom.

As analysts know very well, even when this meaning is discovered the symptom often resists and a part of it remains outside meaning. This brings us to what I have called Lacan's second topography.

The real unconscious and structure

This unconscious remains outside the symbolic and therefore outside meaning and truth. The signifiers, the S_1, have some degree of importance in it, but not so much as part of the signifying chain but rather in terms of their *motérialité* (Lacan's play on *mot*, "word", and *materiality*). In other words, as swarms of sonorous S_1, without meaning, remainders of what the infant had heard and what had an effect on the living matter of this body, the experiences of jouissance linked to maternal care. As Colette Soler writes in *Lacan Reading Joyce*:

> At the structural level, the presence of the child in the adult comes from the fact that what has been inscribed in a contingent manner becomes necessity, never ceasing to write itself. This is what occurs in the repetition of trauma, and also in the symptom-*fixion's* indelibility in the Real of jouissance. ... When we receive an analysand, generally the knot is already there, "already made," as Lacan put it. ... Whence the idea that, at best, through the signifying production of analysis, we will be able to correct the knot with various sutures and splices. ... The analyst ... does not produce the *sinthome*. It was already there, contrary to what one sometimes hears.
>
> (Soler, 2018)

What can we say about the "it was already there"? First of all, with the sinthome, we are no longer dealing with the Borromean link composed of three rings, but with a knot with four rings. Let's remember the three-ring link (see Figure 4.6), with the different failures in the link in psychosis, where either the symbolic or the imaginary slips away.

Ultimately, in the four-ring link, the three orders of the imaginary, symbolic, and real can simply be lying on top of each other or crossing each other. What holds them together is the sinthome as the fourth ring.

The sinthome can be a nomination, the Name-of-the-father, which is already there for the neurotic, structurally present, we might say. Meaning is there and abundantly so. Analysis consists in journeying through meaning towards non-sense. The sinthome might be what the compensated psychotic produces for himself, when the link is not originally there. This production can be of variable quality, more or less reliable, more or less solid, but, in any case, something to be supported and respected. Finally, if there has been a decompensation, it means that the fourth ring did not hold very well and a suppletion must be constructed, something akin to a prosthesis, to a prosthetic sinthome.

Ultimately, the analyst's and analysand's roadmap in neurosis and psychosis is relatively clear, albeit not easy to follow. However, this is not the case for autists, because autism is not a nosographic entity and specially not a purely psychogenic one.

In my view, we should think of the autistic syndrome as a trans-structural construction that is erected on top of an underlying structure, covering or even

Figure 4.6 Figure 4.7

concealing it, each time there is an impediment or an impossibility of entering alienation, regardless of whether the obstacle is organic or linked to the signifying coordinates of one's history (I have given up on using the term "superstructure", which seems to create confusion, especially among Lacanian analysts who tend to hear "super" structure rather than "what is on top").

Impediment and impossibility are not the same thing. An impediment does not mean that the situation might not change, either in the direction of an original psychosis or underlying neurosis. An impossibility is of the order of the real, the fixed nature of which must be taken into account. Because of these two modalities, finding a roadmap for an autistic subject is not easy.

For the neurotic, the trajectory is from the excess of meaning of the symptom towards non-sense. For the non-decompensated psychotic, the work consists in supporting the sinthome the subject has put together for himself or, if there has been a decompensation, helping them construct a suppletion. For the autists, everything depends on the underlying structure, which often only appears at the end of the journey. Even though there is no roadmap, there are a few pointers regarding the analyst's position in the transference and the way of handling interventions and interpretations, as well as a need to be highly inventive and adaptable while working within a very constrained relationship.

The analyst must first of all take seriously the persecution he represents as an other, especially the signs of his presence, which are mostly conveyed by speech (in the choice of signifiers that should be used or avoided), voice (especially in terms of its volume or modulation, for example by singing), by the gaze, but also by the touch. We have to let ourselves be guided by the child: with an "empty" and silent child, we might need to engage in a kind of resuscitation, a "breathing in" of the signifier, while with a child who is invaded by the jouissance and persecution of language or the voice, we might need to opt for a "silent cure".

But beyond that, with all children who are persecuted by the all-powerful real Other we have to avoid any kind of superego injunction resembling an interdiction, an order and so on: "no, don't do that, stop it, etc".

In moments when the jouissance or aggressiveness against other people (in this instance the analyst) or objects should be reduced, or where the child tries to destroy the setting, it is preferable to position oneself as an other with one's own desires, reminding the child of one's existence as an other outside him, a person with his own wishes, joys and pains. This helps cancel out the attempt at nullifying the other: "I don't want you to hurt me. I don't agree with... Do you want us to tidy up? Shall we stop now?" and so on.

Here we should remember the subject's difficulties with separation: in each session, it is better to speak about it in advance. The analyst can let himself be represented by an object that the child can take with him to the waiting room or even home, on the condition that he brings it back next time. This helps avoid the unbearable "hole" in the immutability of the setting (at least at the beginning of the treatment). We can also make use of the presence of the maternal or paternal Other somewhere else, in another place (for example in the waiting room): "Come, let's go see Mommy or Daddy?"

Finally, there is a way of being present without saturating the child with our presence. Some authors have spoken about autists as hyper-sensorial subjects, who perceive sounds, looks, and touch much more strongly than the rest of us do, as a kind of sensory bombardment. This observation is clinically accurate, but its cause should be put in question, given that this type of sensory hyper-responsiveness usually disappears once transference and trust have been established. Because the voice, gaze, and touch are, prior to being objects *a*, the signs of the Other's presence, of his existence in the *Umwelt*, of his radical heterogeneity vis-à-vis the subject's *Innenwelt*, it is better to try not to "bombard" the patient – if indeed we wish to use this expression – with sensations, in order to help them integrate them. For example, we may avoid speaking to them while looking at them directly or touching them, or looking at them and speaking to them at the same time. In "normal" communication, people use gestures to emphasise their speech; their gaze can reassure, validate the listener, indicate that "yes, I am speaking to *you*". With the autistic subject, this should be completely avoided. We should speak to them indirectly, positioning ourselves next to them rather than face to face, or letting them observe us in silence, because sometimes they do look at us, usually rather fixedly and seriously. We can remain with them in a supportive and attentive way, but while doing something else. This "sideways" presence (*être de biais*) seems to me the best definition of the analyst's position.

Simply put, we should adopt a way of being, a position that says: "I am here if you want me to be, to the extent that you can bear it, and I can tolerate the fact that my existence is difficult for you, even though I will not let my existence or otherness be denied." It means not trying to impose oneself, but neither to disappear or consent to being merely an object or a tool, or part of the autistic child. For example, if the child uses my arm to open a drawer so that I may grab something or give him something, I put myself on the scene, I become involved through speech, articulating what it is that he is doing or making me do. In speaking, I am no longer his tool: I introduce a distance.

All interpretation must happen in this context. What is an interpretation? It is adding certain signifiers, our own, to the subject's signifiers, whether they are articulated and clearly announced by him or not. We are adding signifiers to produce an act, so that the subject is not the same before and after – this is the very definition of the act.

Hence we understand the true weight of these few words and how intrusive they can be for a subject who completely refuses to become alienated in the Other's signifiers. All the more so because the reaction of these children to interpretation, whether it leads to a pacification or an explosion, can be very strong and is often immediate.

Therefore, all the above-mentioned safety precautions, in terms of being by their side, of this sideways presence, should be applied even more strictly to interpretation. Again, it should reinforce the following message: "I am not asking you for anything, not even a dialogue or taking turns in responding". To do this, we can also lighten our words by interrupting the normal pace of speech, for example, through humming, speaking in a funny rhythm and so on.

In her well-known case of "Little Dick" – who, by the way, shows all signs of autism – Melanie Klein does not give her famous interpretation, i.e. the big train is Daddy and the station is Mommy, to the child directly. She is not speaking to him. She announces it as if she was talking to herself, as a kind of commentary, almost an aside: "You can take it or leave it, exactly as you wish." I will now try to illustrate my argument with some clinical examples.

First clinical vignette

A, aged four, with beautiful blonde hair, had no language and suffered from violent anxiety attacks, during which she would bite her hands, scratch herself, and fall to the ground. These crises interrupted her apparently empty existence; there were no activities, no gaze or relationship with others. Faced with this emptiness, I began to try to fill it in by putting words to everything: herself, myself, what she was doing or what I was doing at any given moment. "You remember, A, you are four-and-a-half years old – you have come to see me today – oh look, you're moving your hand – yes, that's a doll – do you want to take it? – do you want me to give it to you?" – and so on. Speaking to myself like a madman. I was trying to "inject" the signifier.

Well, it worked, at least to some extent: the child woke up, became involved in a few activities, a few signifiers appeared and, most importantly, the self-destructive anxiety attacks nearly disappeared. As if the capture by the signifiers, the fact of putting words to every activity and thing, made the world exist by subjecting it to the signifiers of the Other. This had a pacifying effect for A, at the cost of a forced signifying "injection". After having been diagnosed with Rett's syndrome, A was sent to a specialised centre and given a poor prognosis, the clinicians refusing to see that underneath a neurologically perturbed organism there may indeed be a subject.

Second clinical vignette

Y had a completely different relationship to language and particularly to *lalangue*. He was of the same age as A, but presented as hyperanimated, jumpy, constantly gesticulating, dancing around, and, above all, singing. He would literally never stop singing, or rather chanting, incomprehensible words, but repeating certain phonematically identifiable sequences (e.g. *atik, keti, ke, tac*...). What was especially remarkable was how intoxicating this production seemed to be: he would get more and more excited and eventually explode in a kind of persecutory jouissance, a fit of screaming, crying and aggressiveness directed both at himself and others. Once the excitation had been discharged, he would return to his default state and begin singing again.

Very quickly I noticed that any intervention through speech, regardless of who it was coming from, had zero pacifying effect and instead only intensified Y's screams. Then, once the intoxication by his signifiers – which were known to him alone and had no signifiers that could be shared with other mortals – had reached its peak, it would trigger a new fit. I also learnt that the psychologist he had seen previously tried to sing and scream with him, which would induce in Y a state of excitation and distress lasting for several hours. I therefore decided to try to communicate to him that I had understood his intolerance of words and sounds by staying silent, or nearly so. At most, I used monosyllabic words. The result was spectacular: in just a week's time, Y calmed down. He might sometimes arrive angry or anxious (for example if his father had refused to give him some treat) and leave calm and happy after this "silent cure", during which we communicated by looks, gestures, and silent demands. Later, when he was not happy because I might have refused him something, he would calm down by asking me for a cuddle, or letting himself relax in my arms for a brief moment. Very slowly, I reintroduced my voice, or let Y play with a tambourine, without his joy or satisfaction turning into a destructive jouissance. He began to devise increasingly more complex games, while I had to stay at the sideline. His language remained autistic; it only became speech on two occasions, both linked to the oral drive. (1) He used modelling clay to make a cake and stuck a marker in it as a candle. He began to sing "Happy Birthday". (2) He sat in front of the drawer where he knew I kept some sweets, saying "sweetie" and then "sweetie Y".

At the age of three, this was all he had in terms of speech, together with "pee" and "mine". However, in terms of behaviour, relationality, and practical skills he had made brilliant progress. As for biological tests, everything always came back negative. The relationship with his mother was characterised by coldness, rigidity, and anger, while it was impossible to say whether this was a cause or a consequence. In addition, the mother would systematically ignore anything the father would say.

The cases of A and Y exemplify two different strategies a subject can use to radically refuse signifying alienation, to maintain himself and his body outside it.

For A, there was a radical separation from language, a refusal to manipulate it, lest she felt herself emptied out by it, sucked into the void, with an inexistent body and ego. Perhaps we could speculate that her attacks, the scratching and biting, were an attempt at existing, at filling in this void and even producing the S_1 on her body. My function as the idiot churning over certain signifiers therefore served to produce certain S_2, to articulate her productions to mine and in this way literally "fill in", filling *her* in and producing a body for her, a body made of words. This would explain the pacifying effect.

In Y's case, there was also a refusal of signifying alienation, a refusal to become alienated in and appropriate the other's signifiers (he had none when we first met), but his refusal to enter into common language resulted in creating his own *lalangue*, his own signifiers and, furthermore, his own rhythms and musicality. While he was in signifiers, these were only his own S_1, non-alienated in the Other's signifiers, and this provoked a kind of mad jouissance. Our attempts to empty this jouissance by our own signifiers or enter into his world in order to share his jouissance were experienced as completely persecutory and invasive, thus only fuelling his anxiety. Emptying this jouissance of signifiers in their rawest, most material form, by withdrawing my voice, could therefore only happen through silence, the "silent cure" as I have called it. Here too there was a pacifying effect, despite – or thanks to – adopting the exact opposite as a strategy.

Third clinical vignette

I saw K, aged two years and two months, at the request of his mother, who was worried by his lack of speech and problematic behaviour. The period of pregnancy was full of conflict: the mother had decided to get pregnant and said nothing to K's father until she was three months along, which he did not appreciate. As a gambler and alcoholic, K's father had "other priorities". The conflicts between the parents continued after K's birth, including father's visit to the A&E because of his wife's violence. The birth was a difficult one and eventually a caesarean was performed due to foetal distress. The child's psychomotor development was more or less normal, but his language quickly petered out. He would say *Papa* and *Mama*, and something like *baba* to ask for a drink or food, but these three little words disappeared after the birth of his younger brother, when K was 15 months old. He showed strong jealousy and aggressiveness towards the new baby for about two months, but then seemed to have decided to ignore his existence. Subsequently he stopped speaking to other people and only spoke to himself, or in any case spoke incessantly in a kind of jargon, a confused mass of sounds that could not be identified or understood. Although he would ignore the Other as a potential addressee of a demand or speech, he maintained good relations with others, in fact with everyone, without distinction: he would take anyone's hand, always happy to follow. In addition, he could switch on the TV or the stereo, change the channel or adjust the volume, and even turn on the father's computer, which he destroyed at the age of two. Lastly, he could not sit still and had little awareness of boundaries and prohibitions. The clinical picture also included severe sleeping problems; he would systematically wake up at night. He refused to eat anything by himself. He was able to become completely absorbed in repetitive activities, such as emptying and filling containers or drawing endless spirals and loops. He refused to go on the potty.

The work proceeded on three levels: obviously with K, but also with his mother, to help her let go of him and let the father have access to him, and finally with his father, so that he could do something about his drinking to actually be able to take care of his children and not to give K's mother an excuse to dismiss him. Very quickly, the relationship between the parents calmed down. They decided that only a separation would be a worthy continuation of their relationship; the disputes died down, though they still had to live together for some time and avoided speaking to each other. The father began to take care of the kids. In fact, it was usually him who brought K to therapy, twice to three times a week, for two and a half years.

K took a long time to settle in, in the literal sense of the word. In the consulting room, he would be like quicksilver. It took him eight months to make his first drawing, a muddle he continued adding to. After several weeks, he first spoke to me, but in his own language; then, a few words from our language appeared: *bonjour, bonsoir, bravo, oui*, and *ordi* ("comp"). After nine months of work, he finally surprised me at the end of a session, saying "Daddy's coming" (*c'est papa qui vient*), showing me that he had in fact a good command of syntax.[4] When he let go of his refusal to speak "like us", he also started going on the potty, accepting to let go of his faeces, and no longer had to wear a nappy.

My work consisted in setting boundaries, by saying what I wanted without confronting him, as opposed to what tended to happen with his mother and provoked his fits. I repeatedly communicated to him: "I don't want you to play with my computer, nor with Daddy's computer." This intervention-interpretation concerned the fact that his father's objects of jouissance were not his own. The work was not finished when K suddenly *disappeared from my screen*: the parents had separated, and the father now lived further away, even though he had the children every weekend. The mother returned to work and felt too overwhelmed to continue bringing K to his sessions. Because of the progress he had made, I decided that things should be alright, and we should better recognise how far he had come. We discussed things with K and I agreed to stop the sessions.

He returned in May 2011. He had spent the last eight months in Reception. He now knew how to read and write, and came back for a speech assessment, due to a few minor sound confusions, which turned out to be fairly ordinary. His problematic behaviour had disappeared; he related to others well. He was happy to see me and to show me what a big boy he had become, his eyes sparkling with mischief. We had two more sessions, six months apart, before and after his work with the speech-therapist, where he had also made good progress and no autistic or psychotic signs were detected. He was not persecuted by the signs of the Other's presence and entered into a mutual relationship without any difficulties. His relation to discourse did not seem in any way altered and no other archaic fantasies were perceptible. His relation to his own body was not symptomatic.

Because I neither claim nor believe in the possibility of "curing" psychosis, or changing anyone's structure full stop, I was forced to conclude that K presented an autistic syndrome or autistic defence mechanisms in the context of an ordinary neurotic structure, as already suggested by my "Oedipoid" interpretation.

Fourth clinical vignette

G was three years and two months old when I first met her. She was born in the United States, to a French mother and an American father, and she returned to France when she was four months old. The mother emphasised that problems had been there right from the start: she was not able to breastfeed the baby and felt uncomfortable. She "didn't know how to go about it and neither did [her daughter]". Kanner notices these early problems of feeding, which later persist (1943, p. 217). At the age of three, G still had to be fed; she would not chew and would spit out bits of food. The only solid food she ate were chocolate biscuits. Initially the parents had feared that she was deaf, because she did not react to her given name. She had only started saying *papa* and *mama* four months previously, and later also her own name. For a period, the only word she used frequently and constantly was *No*, to mark her radical refusal. However, she used her voice as an instrument, continuously vocalising and making barking noises. For some time, she had been repeating everything like an echo (echolalia). In terms of relationships, in the presence of her mother she seemed confident, smiling at everybody, happy to be alive, but could not bear being looked at. As soon as her mother would be gone, she would panic and be overwhelmed by anxiety. As for her body, she had a particularly stiff and slightly robotic gait, sometimes walking on her toes. She also suffered from chronic constipation and often put her fingers into her anus, as if to explore her inner hole, which she would "plug" with her faeces.

The first sessions were difficult; at first, she only agreed to come in with her mother, would be hiding behind her during the entire session and only accepted contact through her. She would only look at me when I was not looking at her, doing her best to prevent our looks from crossing or our bodies from facing each other without her mother's body between us. On these conditions she was charming and babbling, but as if mirroring the other, repeating words and imitating gestures, or making repetitive movements.

One day, she did not say no to my invitation that I see her alone next time. She did not seem convinced, but she consented. On the day, she gave me her hand and followed me like a little lamb; she immediately hid behind the chair where her mother would usually sit and began to cry quietly. The symbolic separation from her mother had not occurred. She experienced physical separation as terribly painful, while the reunion would be joyful. Her crying ceased a little each time I stopped paying attention to her, when I would not try and speak to her. This lasted for several weeks and was only tolerable because G would still seem happy to see me in the waiting room each time I came to fetch her, she was happy to see her mother after each session and sweet when we said goodbye after I'd return her to her mother. Deep down, she was not angry with me for doing my job as a separator; you could say that she consented to it but suffered. We shared this suffering twice a week, same time, same place, but hardly anything else.

And then one day, I found her in the waiting room captivated by some photographs her mother was showing to her: she kept chattering, even naming the people in the pictures. Her mother confirmed that G loved photos and they had found a way of communicating through them. I asked mother to lend me the photos and G and I went into the consulting room. The session was completely different from the previous ones. G sat down next to me and named the different protagonists. Kanner already noticed that "there is a far better relationship with pictures of people than with people themselves. Pictures, after all, cannot interfere" (Kanner, 1943, p. 247). In the following months, I went through the entire family album and got to know everyone in the family, including the grandparents' dog. All this time G was talking to me, taking great care to explain to me who, where, when and so on. The fortress surrendered. Eight months later, G's first drawing shows the fragmented and toric experience of her own body and the body of the other (Figure 4.8).

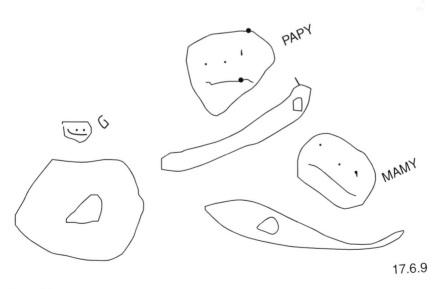

Figure 4.8

The work continued for seven years. I cannot possibly summarise the entire treatment, but I thought it interesting to show G's development and the difficulty of contrasting Kanner's and Asperger's notions of autism given her starting point and where she is now. Two years later, she feels comfortable in her body and draws herself as a whole person (Figure 4.9).

She attended primary school, then junior school. Last summer, I received a letter from her mother, which shows what has changed and what remains the same:

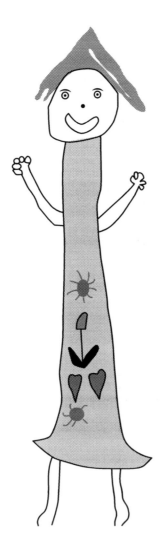

Figure 4.9

Dear Dr Drapier,

You saw G from August 1997 to December 2004 for behavioural problems. You said you would like to know how she's been getting on, so I wanted to give you some news.

This year, G did very well at her baccalaureate (see her grades below!), after studying diligently at her lycée. In September, she is moving to L to study engineering at X ... There were two difficult years in junior school in M ... where she was shunned by a large part of her classmates because of her difference. Nevertheless, she managed to overcome this. However, during her lycée years, we decided she should go and live with her grandparents in M ...

Today she is a very independent young girl, who has kept in touch with all her friends and the world no longer scares her. In August 2011 she spent two weeks in New Zealand as an exchange student. ...

I would like to thank you again for all the help you gave us for such a long time. Who would have thought in 1997 that G would do so well! The work is not over, but we can look toward the future with confidence. ...

Let's complete the picture with G's baccalaureate results, which are quite telling. She took the "Science" stream of the exam and earned a distinction. We see that there are still some problems with language, when it is no longer a simple code and includes equivocation: 20/20 in Physics/Chemistry, 18/20 in Mathematics and English, but 11/20 in French and 7/20 in Philosophy.

To conclude, I would like to say that psychoanalysis has a role to play in both diagnosing and treating autists, but only if we move beyond the simplistic binary of organogenesis versus psychogenesis, the idea of a structural or nosographic unity of a mythic "autism" and the false debate about whose fault it is. On the condition of giving psychoanalysis its rightful place, but not more: a place alongside educators, speech therapists, movement therapists, and others. Autists are a very diverse population and their treatment will therefore necessarily follow multiple paths.

Notes

1 This lecture was first presented during a study day on autists, institutions, psychoanalysts, and some others on 8 October 2016 in Narbonne, organised by the Institution and Psychoanalysis Network of the École de Psychanalyse des Forums du Champ Lacanien. It was published in *Mensuel*, 114, p. 45–63.
2 CRA – *Centre Ressources Autisme*. These state-run regional centres are intended to serve people with autism or their families. They provide screening services, advice, financial help etc.
3 CMPP – *Centre Medico-Psycho-Pédagogique*. The network of these public institutions still constitutes the backbone of the French child mental health system. They usually have a multidisciplinary team headed by a child psychiatrist and offer free consultations and treatments (in some cases still long-term), often a combination of psychotherapy, speech therapy, movement therapy, and other interventions. In the

past, many of these centres offered psychoanalytical or psychoanalytically inspired treatment – sadly today this is no longer the case.
4 Translator's note: In French, the sentence *c'est papa qui vient* is indeed slightly more syntactically complex.

References

Fombonne, E. (2009). Epidemiology of pervasive developmental disorders. *Pediatr Res*, 65(6), 591–598.

Kanner, L. (1943). Autistic disturbance of affective contact. *Nervous Child*, 2, 217–250.

Mahler, M. (1979). *Infantile Psychosis and Early Contributions*. Lanham, MN: Jason Aronson.

Soler, C. (2018). *Lacan Reading Joyce: Reading, Writing and Psychoanalysis*. London: Karnac.

Tustin, F. (1992). *Autistic States in Children*. London: Routledge.

Chapter 5

A psychoanalyst in the land of ABA[1]

Marie-Dominique Amy

It may seem peculiar that a psychoanalyst would be interested in cognitivist methods. However, if we accept the idea that the autistic pathology essentially stems from certain disconnections and splits that undermine all kinds of consubstantiality – corporeal, sensory, mental, and psychic – we might understand that some psychoanalysts would like to know more about how and why these disconnections come about, taking into account both psychodynamic observations, as well as genetic, neurological, and cognitivist research.

When I started working, some 35 years ago, I found myself in one of the many hospital units where the policy of non-direction and of waiting for the emergence of the patient's desire was applied literally. It was terrible: there was no contact between clinicians, no contact with the parents. The latter were forbidden from visiting the day hospital, from meeting the staff and the therapist; they knew nothing about their child's treatment plan – mostly because no such plan existed.

I quickly realised that by using simple words, gestures, and expressions, by making use of what Paul-Claude Racamier has called "speaking actions" (*actions parlantes*) (Racamier, 1990, p. 1177), I could help these patients live better. I was quite successful at relieving these children, with or without language, of some of their anxieties, their sometimes "catastrophic" emotions and the suffering they caused; more generally, I could work with their complex psychic experiences, but I knew nothing about their cognitive difficulties.

However, the basis of the autistic pathology lies essentially in the autist's inability to make connections, to realise that there is a correlation between their feelings and their experience. For a long time, they will moan, laugh, roll on the floor, or behave violently without ever being able, even when they can speak, to tell us what has put them in such a state – for the simple reason that they know absolutely nothing about it themselves.

This bodily-psychic-cognitive dislocation is so disabling that in the 1980s I decided to undergo a training in educational strategies, including alternative, non-verbal communication, but also in diagnostic assessment and specifically the creation of individualised therapy projects. More recently, I have also trained in Applied Behaviour Analysis (ABA), because I had heard all kinds of things about this method and wanted to make my own opinion.

DOI: 10.4324/9781003221487-6

This experience has been of considerable use in helping me observe and understand to what extent certain psychic problems can hinder learning, but also that certain types of learning could put an end to negative behaviour and emotions. That said, we still need to understand and learn how to remedy the disjunctions that prevent autists from making sense of the situations they face and of cause-and-effect relationships, and which impair their ability to generalise.

A necessary remark

These preliminary observations led me to the conclusion that the persisting theoretical conflicts between the psychodynamic and cognitivist approaches only further reinforce the autists' difficulties. They can be of absolutely no use in helping them connect their experience to their emotions. Today's neuroscience highlights the importance of linking the individual's experience with the corresponding emotions. Practically all of this research suggests that environment plays a key role in the quality of neuronal circuits, as amply evidenced by the discoveries related to neuroplasticity (Ansermet & Magistretti, 2004).

Jacqueline Nadel (Nadel & Decety, 2002) has shown that a child who cannot imitate or understand that another is imitating him remains excluded from the world of others. We professionals therefore cannot continue working with autists while always only treating either their psychic state or their bodily, emotional, or cognitive state. By acting out our divisions, we do nothing but reinforce their own.

As for the question of the treatment of autism, we must first keep in mind that although communication, socialisation, and learning are always affected, depending on their individual forms of splitting, different autists have managed their condition in very different ways, according to their degree of impairment, the presence or absence of mental disability, and the somatic issues sometimes associated with autism. They are thus very different from one another and require different objects, forms of mediation, and educational support.

Let's take the example of sensory differences. Some autists only grasp the outside world visually, others through hearing, smell, taste, or touch. Unfortunately, none of these senses are linked together with the others; there is no cross-modal sensory processing. And even though our aim may be to slowly move towards this linking, at the beginning of the treatment we cannot *not* rely on what constitutes the person's most sensitive sensory reference. This means that from the outset we must use highly personalised tools and strategies. Unless we manage to slowly help the person assimilate these necessary sensory crossings, they will remain profoundly excluded from any understanding of what is happening around them. The relationship between the inner and outer world will remain fragmented.

Therefore, I find it absurd when certain institutions try to implement standardised programmes. And yet some parents and professionals, often relying on false statistical data, believe that this is the right way forward.

A double reading

As a psychoanalyst, I have found it puzzling that during some of the cognitivist trainings I attended, certain words were completely taboo. You could not suggest that this or that situation could be experienced by the autistic person as painful. You could not argue that the disturbances of their inner world could have anything to do with their learning difficulties and that certain perceptions, certain severe and archaic anxieties could be at the origin of their abnormal behaviour.

For the hardcore cognitivists – and there are still some out there – everything boils down to the imperative of learning, while the rest does not really count. Yet to be perfectly honest, some psychoanalysts can be equally tenacious when making the opposite argument. In their mind, learning should only be pursued once the person's psychic difficulties have been cleared away. These two extremes resemble each other in the sense that both demonstrate a deep misunderstanding of the fundamental issue in autism, i.e. the inability to link together perceptions, sensations, affects, attention, and memory.

Based on the above, I suggest that we must constantly pursue a *double reading* of the situations experienced by autists, whether it is during assessments, during learning, playing, feeding, etc. Before and during the treatment, we need long periods of observation. Assessments such as PEP 3, AAPEP 4, or EFI 5 can be very helpful, but it is just as important to observe everyday situations, provided that in either of these relational moments we pay attention to both the person's cognitive capacities and the associated emotional reactions.

This double reading can help us take into account the impact of cognition on emotional life and vice versa; this saves us a lot of time and helps us avoid potentially catastrophic errors when the child, adolescent, or adult is confronted with incomprehensible situations or learning formats, with learning sessions that are too long or too short, or with activities that may terrify them.

Although such combined approaches are much more common today, some institutional teams remain reticent as to non-verbal communication and educational strategies. Others think that psychoanalysis is completely useless. These types of resistance are shocking, because they do not respect the autistic person as a whole.

From the educational perspective: at a time when nurseries and maternity schools routinely implement visual tracking systems to help calm down very small children, who are often disturbed by the changes in space or activity – and yet these children are mostly able to learn spontaneously – why do we automatically speak of "robotisation" whenever we try to do the same with autists? Why refuse to give children who do not have the same level of insight reference frameworks that can help them understand us and, more importantly, make themselves understood?

From the perspective of psychoanalysis: why refuse to take into account the autists' difficulties in registering images and ideas, which are indispensable in order for history, space, and time to take shape? I repeat, it is the inability to make these different functional references coexist that is the basis of the difficulties of autism.

What about the ABA method?

What are the benefits, for these children, adolescents, and adults, of psychoeducational methods, the combination of which would be, again, greatly enriched if it also included the psychodynamic approach? In this text, I will focus on the ABA method.

While its goals may be similar to other methods, such as TEACCH – developing autonomy, helping the child adapt to a non-family or institutional environment, removing inappropriate behaviours – its strategy is based on a different principle. We must therefore carefully consider which method may be appropriate in a given case.

Éric Schopler (Schopler et al., 1989), who created the TEACCH programme in the 1960s, essentially wanted to avoid subjecting autists to procedures and environments they could not understand. On the contrary, in order not to waste time the framework had to be adapted to their current possibilities of understanding. The references that were offered to the individual, for example, always had to take into account his or her capacities of linking the object, its image, and the word that designates it. We could therefore argue that the TEACCH method is developmental rather than behavioural, in the sense that it is based on the hypothesis that learning leads to the disappearance of abnormal behaviour.

It seems to me that the premises of ABA are quite different. There is no sense of adapting the environment to the autist's problems of comprehension (even though the sessions take place in a calm and relaxed setting); instead, the goal is to help the person become more fully integrated into an environment that is not to be adjusted to their difficulties. In this sense, we "move away from a culture where the individual is the problem to a culture in which the environment is the problem" (Ghislain Margerotte).

The goals of ABA concern, first of all, the different measures to be implemented so that the person can abandon behaviour that is negative or ill-adapted to this natural environment, behaviour that prevents them from learning and becoming more autonomous. Founded on the behavioural hypotheses developed by Ivar Lovaas in the 1960s, the method was subsequently further developed by different researchers and clinicians (Leaf et al., 1999).

There are two types of teaching in ABA: either (1) a process with very specific objectives and following a fixed programme, the result of a battery of observations, or (2) the so-called "incidental" teaching. The latter tries to help the autistic child, adolescent, or adult learn through spontaneous activities. This teaching can be based on a play activity and practised in a context of joint attention.

When ABA practitioners recognise the importance of combined approaches, when they accept working as part of a team and are able to hear and take into consideration what speech therapists, movement therapists and psychotherapists have to say, and when they themselves are willing to speak to these different professionals about their own practice, we see that the children develop homogenously, peacefully, and in some cases rather spectacularly. However, the "honest" practitioners of ABA also recognise that their approach is not a miracle cure. The journey is long and complete cure is an illusion; here, like anywhere else, failures do occur.

On the other hand, those who take an excessively forceful approach only cause harm to the ABA method. Their version of it looks rather terrifying.

When this approach is used, admittedly tenaciously but in a positive relational context, in a measured way and as joyfully as possible, it can be effective – not for all autists, as some would like to think, but especially for those who are subject to violent and ill-adapted behaviour or to severe regression. Rigour is not rigidity; this teaching approach can be flexible and must take into account the autist's personality. "Reasonable" trainers emphasise this, as well as the fact that complete assimilation is doctrinaire and absurd. No method or strategy can be used in the same way with all autistic people.

ABA often intensely relies on the use of the non-verbal communication method PECS 9 (Picture Exchange Communication System, Frost & Bondy, 2001); the teams that use this method as part of the TEACCH or ABA framework know that it depends, at least in the beginning, on the degree of the person's psychic and mental development.

We could also argue that in many situations the careful use of ABA seems quite sensible. If it is offered in the calm and peaceful setting I have described, it may appear not so dissimilar from what we sometimes do as parents with our own children. However, while we often have to repeat things with children who do not have the difficulties of mental or emotional registration of autistic children, this is all the more necessary or even unavoidable when working with children who face the world in a general state of incomprehension of their experience. Helping them make sense of this experience is therefore an absolute priority. They first need to "install" a number of prerequisites, the point of which they cannot understand: learning how to sit, how to observe, how to participate… They need help acquiring things that the rest of us consider the basic alphabet of living together, because for them, no learning happens spontaneously.

The ABA method is based initially on diagnostic assessments and later on other forms of evaluations needed to create an individualised plan. Before the plan is put in place, it relies on observations of how the child functions in everyday activities, in other words, on their cognitive profile, manifest behaviour, their strengths and weaknesses.

This detailed observation allows us to at first keep to the person's abilities and bypass their weaknesses. Every type of behaviour has its cause and when it is not based on organised thought, as it is the case with autists, it is difficult to control. To create an individual programme, it must first be elaborated and drafted on the basis of certain prerequisites: the initial evaluation of behaviours; their functions; the objectives to be attained; using this or that strategy of intervention; evaluating the level of achieving these objectives. It is also vital to identify, as clearly as possible, the triggers of negative behaviour: when, where, and how often they occur.

We also need to observe and keep in mind whether the person is more comfortable in a one-on-one situation or in a group setting, so as not to put them at a disadvantage. The idea is of course that over time they will become accustomed to being present and able to function in both contexts.

Often these preliminary observations lead the trainers to necessarily prioritise the relevant sensory stimuli, which means trying to help the person make the kinds of connections I spoke about earlier, because for as long as these links do not exist, any learning will necessarily remain partial.

Therefore, for the behaviours and actions to become operational, the autist must first understand the logic of *if-then*. The teachers and parents will try to help them understand the consequences of this or that behaviour or action, which can thus become contingent. The ABA practitioners distinguish between these types of operant behaviour and "respondent conditioning", considered a reflex behaviour. They nevertheless emphasise that working with such reflex conditioning can be useful in the case of certain phobias.

They also stress that we cannot wait for the autist to begin to "wish to" do something (which again echoes the utopian expectation of certain psychoanalysts of a certain era, namely that a desire emerges) and that during the time of learning, we cannot leave them the choice of either doing something or not. This obviously does not mean that the notion of choice should not also be meaningful, quite the contrary. Because of the autists' difficulties in understanding the goals and larger functions of an action or learning, ABA practitioners use something called forward or backward *chaining*. Either the learner is taught to complete each step of the sequence to reach the goal, or they start from the outcome and proceed backwards.

All this requires that the teachers must regularly evaluate their propositions, identifying whether their implementation has resulted in a positive modification or not. Another priority is to help the person learn to have a better life – helping them understand that the disappearance of certain behaviours positively impacts their relationships with others and with their environment in general, which is essential. In order for the person to be able to generalise from these new acquisitions, it is important that neither of them is taught by a single person. The child must learn to manage these learning acquisitions in different contexts and with different teachers – the father, the mother, etc.

Because of these hypotheses, of the autists' lack of understanding of situations, cause-and-effect relationships, and the functions of objects and situations, the learners have to be stimulated. Teaching in a situation to which the child seems sensitive, using a game or an object, is key – if this does not happen, the contact, relationship, and success are imperilled.

Given the enormous difficulty or even impossibility of autists to spontaneously understand if-when relationships and, a fortiori, to analyse what they are faced with, the "founders" of the ABA method developed so-called "reinforcements". These should bring satisfaction, a reward for a successful action; they can be verbal, manual, or behavioural. In their view, this is the first and indispensable stage of meaning-making, the first step in helping the autistic person experience success. Once the cause-and-effect relationship of this accomplishment seems clear, they try to eliminate the reinforcement. They explain that punishment seems inappropriate and therefore useless.

Reinforcements can be highly varied and of course depend on the mental level of the person receiving them, but also on their interests. For the most regressed autists this can be communicated in the form of food; for those who enjoy social reinforcements, it can be praise ("bravo, fantastic, more…"), or it can be an object the person is interested in. More generally, these so-called "positive" reinforcements try to help the autistic person make the link between a certain behaviour, task, or experience and pleasure. However, a "positive" reinforcement can become negative in its effects, if it enables the autistic person to avoid a task he is asked to perform or a situation he finds disagreeable. In this case, the child, adolescent, or adult will quickly understand that by choosing inappropriate behaviour, he will get what he wants, namely escaping the task required. This will only lead to a repetition of the process. Hence the trainer must be careful not to offer reinforcements that lead to evasive behaviour. I will not go into detail about all the types of reinforcement and how they are chosen; however, the trainers explain that for a reinforcement to have an impact on a given behaviour or a task, it must follow very quickly. Waiting for too long annuls its benefits. Still, regardless of the nature of the reinforcement, the trainer's goal is to eventually eliminate it completely, once the pleasure of succeeding or the wellbeing obtained have become sufficient in themselves. In other words, it requires the appearance of the idea of contingency I have spoken about earlier.

What are the possible connections between ABA and psychoanalysis?

Without trying to reach a weak consensus at any cost, we could argue that under certain conditions, concerning the ways in which ABA is administered, some points of connection can and should be established. We find them in the emphasis on flexibility, relationality, and playfulness, on the careful observation and attention given to what the autist himself shows to us. However, while psychoanalysis listens to the latent content beneath what can be observed, ABA does not take this into account. While for the former, analysing behaviour relies largely on the emotions, anxieties, affects, and psychic malaise to be deciphered, for the latter it is only the consequence of resisting or avoiding unpleasant situations, which has to do with conditioning or deconditioning, again based purely on what can be observed. Under these conditions, the underlying emotions count for very little and none of the aspects of the interaction that have to do with transference will be analysed.

However, if these two axes can be seen as complementary, they can be of considerable use in helping the autistic person achieve structuration in a holistic manner.

This goes back to the recent research on neuroplasticity. Studies have shown that the synaptic transmission between neurones is highly dependent on the subject's emotional experience. Every individual is thus unique in his own way. And when Freud speaks about the *mnesic trace*, does he not come to the same conclusion? Does he not show us that our earliest sensations, the perceptions that give rise to emotions and affects, are what makes us unique human beings, different from one another?

If we accept that no experience is exempt from emotions, it becomes difficult to imagine that these neuronal and psychic traces would be moving alongside each other without ever crossing. These encounters or intersections, which neuroscientific research has found evidence for, mean that we can no longer ignore their importance. Based on the data on neuroplasticity, we can therefore speculate that what the autistic person suffers from is linked to the fact that producing these connections and intersections is extremely difficult.

If we also agree that, in order to overcome the confinement of autism, the autistic child, adolescent, or adult needs to become more autonomous in order to live, as well as possible, in some kind of collective with others, we must accept that there are arguments for subjecting them to intensive psychoeducational work, in order to try to bring together what initially appears as completely disarticulated. This also means helping them make the links necessary to any attempts at communication, in order to understand both the nature of their own emotions and those of others, and obtain a basic degree of autonomy.

In my own experience, when young autists reach adolescence and this high-risk period again brings to the surface massive regressions and/or behaviours we often thought they had already overcome, those who have previously benefited from the psycho-cognitivist methods go through this time with much less upset. Of course we cannot generalise, but we often see that they are better at managing and analysing their drive-related anxieties when they can express them in a climate of trust.

Supervising teams who deal with older adolescents and young adults, who are often in very poor psychological state, has only strengthened my belief that we must begin working with autistic children as early as possible. Some of these patients have not been able to learn very much at all. They are not toilet-trained, they cannot feed themselves, they may be violent or even dangerous, and have little or no verbal comprehension. They were not given any strategies or tools to help them understand others and make themselves understood. This state of things makes me incredibly angry, because I see it as the terrible legacy of our professional disagreements and divisions. An individualised treatment plan should be set up as early as possible, as soon as the diagnosis has been made, and taking into account the bodily, sensory, cognitive and psychic difficulties of the child in question. This plan should be agreed on by the parents and the clinicians; it goes without saying that such consensus does not alter or modify their particular skills. However, the goals need to be shared and each person needs to respect and take into consideration what their colleagues and also the parents are doing.

A need for openness

Based on what I have just said, a simple conclusion seems insufficient. Instead, I wish to speak about openness, modelled on what many parents already do spontaneously. When they take care of their child, they are not asking whether they are raising him, educating him, making him more independent, teaching him about hygiene, rules, and prohibitions. Neither do they ask whether or not they should consider the emotions this provokes in themselves and in the child.

Cognitive psychology is trying to construct the interindividual dimension, while psychoanalysis aims at the intersubjective. We all know that one does not exist without the other. Without their articulation, their entanglement, there can be no empathy – and empathy is the hardest skill for autists to acquire.

The respect we all owe to them requires that we approach their difficulties holistically. We need to stop cutting them into pieces. Neither side can expect to produce a miracle, but by working together and respecting each other we can offer our patients the very best we can do.

There are no miracles to expect from either the ABA method or the TEACCH programme, or from any other psychoeducational strategy. But when they are carried out in the context of a relationship, flexibly, skilfully, and intelligently, they are necessary or even indispensable. An increasing number of trainers relying on these strategies have understood the need for and the helpfulness of a combined approach.

When these conditions are met, we see how rewarding they are for both sides and how important for the patients we treat. We can even argue that they help them develop more quickly and above all more homogenously, in a more reassuring and containing manner. There is no longer a risk of robotisation or using insensitive behaviour. Let's hope that in the near future, we will finally understand how harmful some of these conflicts are and that in the field of treating autism we can certainly do better.

Note

1 The original version of this article was published in *Enfances & Psy*, 46(1): 82–93.

References

Amy, M-D. (2004). *Comment aider l'enfant autiste*. Paris: Dunod.
Amy, M-D. (2008). *Construire et soigner la relation mère-enfant*. Paris: Dunod.
Ansermet, F. & Magistretti, P. (2004). *À chacun son cerveau*. Paris: Odile Jacob.
Frost, L.A. & Bondy, A.S. (2001). Picture exchange communication system. *Behavior Modification*, 25(5), 725–744.
Leaf, R. & McEachin, J. (1999). *A Work in Progress: Behavior Management Strategies and a Curriculum for Intensive Behavioural Treatment of Autism*. New York: Different Roads to Learning.
Nadel, J. & Decety, J. (2002). *Imiter pour découvrir l'humain*. Paris: PUF.
Racamier, P-C. (1990). En psychanalyse et sans séance. *Revue française de psychanalyse*, 54(5), 1165–1184.
Schopler, E., Reichler, R.J. & Lansing, M. (1989). *Stratégies éducatives de l'autisme*. Paris: Masson.

Chapter 6

Psychoanalysis for autisms

Patrick Landman

The claim that psychoanalysis is dead to autisms is based on several corroborating facts. First, after the 1960s and 1970s, when the field of child psychiatry was more or less dominated by psychoanalytic theories, the subsequent 30 years saw a paradigm shift towards neuroscience and behaviourist theories. All the exceptional contributions of psychoanalysis – its fine clinical observations, subtle descriptive models, and hypotheses on psychic functioning, especially the defence mechanisms of autism such as adhesive identification – were overtaken by the new neuroscience perspective.

Already the direct infant observation experiments carried out by Brazelton et al. (1974), Bower (1974), or Trevarthen (1979) and following Esther Bick's model led to a revision of certain concepts, such as the "normal primary autism" described by Frances Tustin (1922), thus distinguishing the autistic condition from an archaic stage of normal development with a fixation or regression. No such normal primary autistic stage exists: the rigorous observations of new-born babies have shown this unambiguously. Rather than primary autism, there seems to be a core of primary intersubjectivity, but this does not necessarily predict or determine the entrance into secondary intersubjectivity, i.e. coming into contact with an other constituted as an object distinct from ourselves. Certain exogenous environmental elements, including the interaction with the baby's caregivers, or endogenous, e.g. cerebral, factors may preclude the movement from this primary core to secondary intersubjectivity. Some (Golse, 2013) have made a link between the absence of sensory co-modalisation in autism (the impossibility of integrating two sensory fluxes) and the assembling/dismantling leading to the constitution of the external object (Meltzer, 1972). This revision had an important consequence: autism could no longer fit into the Freudian or Kleinian categories of psychic development, such as polymorphous perversion for perversions (Freud, 1905, p. 190) or the paranoid-schizoid or depressive position for the psychoses (Klein, 1946). At this point, psychoanalysts could have moved from an explanatory model to a more modest and purely descriptive model, but this was not the case. First, some did not recognise Tustin's amendments, rejecting the conclusions of direct observation on the basis of their own clinical

DOI: 10.4324/9781003221487-7

experience. Tustin herself continued to speak about "psychogenic autism", taking as her reference the post-traumatic stress disorder with its fixation on "not knowing, not understanding". In her view, in psychogenic autism there was a traumatic awareness of a separation from the mother; it was an amplification or an exaggeration, an intensification of a set of reactions specific to trauma, a mechanism of psychic survival.

While the clinical cases described by some of these analysts are rather convincing, the hypotheses underpinning the idea of psychogenic autism have never been corroborated by neuroscience findings. However, it is a well-known fact that even risky, approximate or downright false theories can sometimes bring about a "cure". It is quite clear that some cases of autism are correlated with traumatic trajectories such as early abandonment, with all kinds of neglect and sometimes even iatrogenic, i.e. medical abuse committed during hospitalisations during the first months of a baby's life. However, this is obviously not the general rule and correlation does not equal causality, meaning that traumatic elements can act as a trigger in the presence of neurological or genetic vulnerability, but the causal chain remains unknown. These traumatising events have the same function as certain metabolic or genetic illnesses, encephalopathies or epilepsies, which are associated with autistic syndromes, with what we call "syndromic autisms", as opposed to "prototypical autisms", which are unrelated to any other identifiable brain pathology. These associated diseases can perhaps trigger the autistic syndrome, which would make these forms of autism a kind of "final common pathway" for a whole range of pathologies. In other words, we should speak of *autisms* in the plural, instead of autism in the singular.

The problem is compounded by the most recent genetic findings, according to which nearly 40% of cases of autism have a genetic origin. However, this is almost never a question of a single gene and in most cases we see a complex picture of multiple mutations on multiple genes, of which each has a very low penetrance. It is only their association that counts, but is not sufficient, because their phenotypic expression cannot be determined in advance. In other words, the same mutations can result in both autism and another pathology, or in no pathology at all. Their clinical interest lies in the fact that in the case of a clinical picture of autism related to an accidental "de novo" mutation, parents who would like to have another child do not a priori have anything to worry about, which is different in the case of a transmitted mutation. Simply put, there is no "autism gene". Genetic mutations are also mostly relevant to syndromic autisms and for the moment much less so to prototypical autisms; to put this otherwise, the "purer" the autism, the less "genetic" it is, or at least that is the current scientific position.

The second large series of reasons to explain the "death" of the psychoanalytic approach to autism has to do with autism's new definition in the DSM. After eliminating infantile psychosis and initially including autism in the so-called *pervasive developmental disorders* (PDD), starting from the fifth version of the Manual there has been a shift to the *autism spectrum disorders* (ASD). In other words, autism has become the central reference: patients are "more or less" autistic and autism itself is defined based on relatively simple criteria. This has made it possible to lower the thresholds of inclusion, resulting in an incredible rise in prevalence. Soon we are all going to be autistic.

Only two diagnostic criteria suffice for inclusion on the spectrum: (1) "Persistent deficits in social communication and social interaction across multiple contexts." Communication and social interaction have been grouped together in DSM-5, while they had been kept separate in DSM-IV. (2) "Restricted, repetitive patterns of behaviour, interests, or activities" (DSM-5, American Psychiatric Association, 2013).

If these two criteria check out, we can start making a diagnosis of ASD. This will then be confirmed or refuted by additional tests and assessments, but the first step has already been taken and this inclusion on the spectrum according to the DSM criteria is taken into account in the calculations of prevalence. The latter can be used in political lobbying to obtain funding for care institutions, research, and different types of aid. The diagnosis of autism also gives the child and his family legal access to specific benefits and thus carries certain advantages compared to other diagnoses.

The diagnosis of ASD is essentially based on observing behaviour; it can therefore naturally lead to a therapeutic approach that is exclusively behaviourist. It highlights the deficits and ignores the child's capabilities – this too encourages or follows the spirit of purely normative methods. Yet the majority of autistic people have significant abilities. It is therefore highly debatable whether we should consider their limited range of interests from a purely negative standpoint, trying to prevent them from pursuing them, when in fact they might represent a curiosity about or an awakening to the outside world, of collecting data or searching for information. This perspective is promoted by the advocates of neurodiversity such as Laurent Mottron (2016). However, the diagnostic criteria of the DSM are not at all interested in the psychic reality of autistic people, e.g. in the periodical manifestations of what could be seen as strong paroxysmal anxieties. This psychic reality is simply outside the picture.

The DSM dealt the final blow to psychoanalysis in the field of autism by designating autism as a neuro-developmental disorder. It is not the term itself that is the problem but the aetiological interpretations it leads to. "Neuro-developmental" evokes neurology and thus a mono-factorial, purely organic aetiology, a certain – if not definite – determinism, a return to the medicine of the organ, the brain, and excluding all psychic causality since the psyche is not an organ.

Finally, the social perception of autism has also changed thanks to the actions of psychiatric users and autists themselves, who have increasingly been turning away from not just psychoanalysis but also from psychiatry, accusing both of apportioning blame, of incarceration and stigmatisation. They refuse to be seen as mentally ill, which is understandable. Some consider autism as just another singular way of being. Because we are all different, we also have different brains; some individuals are neuro-typical, others, such as autists, are neuro-atypical. This perspective has led to the formation of a community united by its autistic identity. In 1943, autism was a very serious pathology, with little hope for change; in 2017, it is a way of being just like any other, one whose voice should be heard and included in our society.

There is little point in criticising this development, unless we want to appear nostalgic for the past, the golden age of psychoanalysis and psychiatry, which was in fact very far from perfect. In France, autistic people and their parents were too often faced with a certain arrogance of psychoanalysts, an attitude which in fact concealed an inability to provide a cure, and with the dominant doxa which located the original sin in the parental and especially maternal desire, a belief that could only be understood as apportioning blame. I wonder if this was not the influence of religion on the analytic doxa, replacing Eve's original sin in Genesis with the original sin of the autistic child's mother. Nonetheless, it often resulted in additional trauma: bringing a child to the consultation who is very different from others and difficult to interact with, and then being indirectly accused of having been the cause of his pathology only deepens the injury. This type of trauma is so widespread that many parents prefer the intensive behaviourist methods such as ABA, which reduce them to a teaching assistant at the expense of any spontaneity and parental initiative, often making them feel guilty for the slightest diversion off course. In fact, the psychoanalysts who work specifically in the field of autism today are aeons away from the practices that the user groups continue to denounce. The very idea of interpreting an autistic symptom the way Freud interpreted hysteria at the beginning of the 20th century is utter nonsense, an absurdity, and today's analysts work with autists in a completely different way. In our time, the psychoanalytic treatment of autism is part of a multi-disciplinary action programme, which includes educational, pedagogical, and re-educational methods, in addition to speech-therapy, movement therapy, and others.

Lastly, the psychoanalytic doxa that "blamed" parents for their child's condition has left a very surprising legacy. Some parents of autists and some users argue that these beliefs have had an influence on social workers who advocate taking autistic children into care. In reality, the question arises if an autistic child regularly presents with bruises, wounds, and haematoma. Is this a case of self-mutilation or abuse? Obviously, the answer can only be given case by case, while keeping in mind that self-mutilation does occur and can give rise to suspicions of abuse; it is up to the professionals to know how to tell them apart. The parents of autists are men and women like any others and are in no way to blame for their child's autism; they have to deal with a very complex and difficult interaction, which creates psychic suffering that must be taken into consideration. The parents of autists should neither be diabolised nor blamed; yet neither should they be made into saints and some cases of abuse may indeed occur. However, blaming psychoanalysis for cases in which a child was taken into care unjustifiably is irrational and indeed abusive.

Long live the psychoanalysis of autisms!

What have psychoanalysts done to resist these trends?

After all that I have just said, one could object that psychoanalysis no longer has its place in the treatment of autism, that it has turned out to be a flawed method which confuses autisms with psychosis, claims that autism has psychogenic aetiology, and so on. And yet psychoanalytic treatment has turned out to be effective, as evidenced by hundreds of case studies and dozens of books. These case studies are not taken into account by scientific experts, who only consider randomised double-blind or similar clinical trials as scientific proof – the famous rule of the medical consensus, the "offspring" of evidence-based medicine (EBM). Many books and articles have demonstrated the limits of EBM in general and in psychiatry especially, but no matter, no better decision guidelines have been found. Case studies are of course far from perfect; they are potentially biased, because the assessor and the therapist are the same person, there is no control group and the progress attributed by the therapist to the therapy of, for example, an autistic child can also be seen as a spontaneous evolution of the pathology or as due to other factors. Case studies cannot be reproduced, as science would dictate. For all these reasons, the cases of psychoanalytic treatments with autists do not fit into the framework of the consensus of experts, who are tasked in all European countries with the publication of good practice recommendations, which are more or less binding for practitioners. This fact marginalises psychoanalysis and is the reason why following the publication, by the American Psychological Association, of the rules for the "scientific" assessment of psychotherapies, some psychoanalysts have established research protocols that take into account the specificity of psychodynamic therapy with autists. The intermediate outcomes are interesting and encouraging; for example, it has been observed that the general characteristics of the adapted clinical practice of mostly psychoanalytic practitioners (58 out of 65) in no way resemble the widespread caricatures of psychoanalysis. At the same time, these clinicians share certain characteristics: sensitivity, dedication, a way of prioritising the patient and making subtle adjustments to accommodate his needs; the ability to tolerate the provocations and violent impulses of certain children; making use of the pre-verbal dimension, etc. The participation and support of parents are of course also key aspects of this work (Thurin et al., 2014).

Hence, psychoanalysts who treat autists, or at least some of them, have decided to participate in research that also applies to other therapeutical methods, especially pharmacological. The results have already been subject to criticism and controversy, but they do exist.

Psychoanalysts have resisted not just the game of evaluation; their resistance has also been "aetiological". The consensus definition of autism as a neuro-developmental disorder can be contrasted with another definition, of autism as "the most severe form of the failure of intersubjectivity". Putting emphasis on intersubjectivity rather than neuro-developmental aspects opens up new perspectives, because access to intersubjectivity is gained gradually, over multiple stages during which the relationship with close others, primarily the parents, is essential. The classic psychic causality is replaced by interactive causality. Psychoanalytic treatments highlight this aspect of access to intersubjectivity; in this sense, psychoanalysis is irreplaceable. We observe that during the first year of life, infants can show signs of the autistic spectrum, but not all of them will develop autism; some of them will withdraw into the autistic syndrome, while others return to a normal course of development. Some psychoanalysts have therefore spoken about an "autisticizing process" (*processus autistisant*) (Hochmann, 1990), in which we can intervene to divert its course from heading towards a full-fledged autistic syndrome. Not everything is decided at birth; multiple factors can intervene in this process, specifically in the child's interaction with his caretakers. Hence the idea that a psychoanalyst can use his observation and clinical experience to help parents interact with a child in difficulty.

Family videos recorded as part of an Italian research study have shown, for example, that interactions between a hypotonic baby, who communicated and responded very little, and was thus at risk of developing autism, and a hyperstimulating mother were often counterproductive. Working on the interaction between a child at risk of autism and the adults, while trying to encourage an opening towards intersubjectivity, means taking an approach contrary to the ABA-type methods, which only look at interaction in terms of behaviour, where parents are given the role of teaching assistants and the ABA rules must be followed everywhere and at all times.

Among the numerous criticisms made against psychoanalysis we also hear that it is not sufficiently active, with the analyst waiting for the child's desire to emerge. This leaves the child in the autistic world for too long and interferes with his development, reducing opportunities for growth. This criticism is underpinned by the idea that brain development happens in stages, like an open window; if the opportunity is not seized, the window closes, and learning becomes much more difficult if not impossible. In reality, this seems to only be the case for certain types of learning, such as learning how to read, but not for others. While it is true that the psychoanalytic treatment of autistic children requires the therapist to exercise a certain degree of restraint, it is never undertaken without the child also receiving other, active or more active types of care. Plus, the educational techniques based on stimulation and play, which are based on the child's desires, seem effective for young children. We should stress that the recent scientific discoveries do not in the least discredit the use of relational treatment or play therapy.

For example, the recent Prix INSERM laureate Professor Catherine Barthélémy has developed, together with Professor Gilbert Lelord, the *Exchange and Development Therapy*, a play therapy practised as part of a multi-approach care model (twice weekly) at a day hospital. Dr Barthélémy argues that the quality of life of autists is improved "in any case" by "helping them gain confidence, promoting exchange, bonding with and relating to others" (*La Croix*, 6 December 2016).

The *Denver method* (ESDM) has received much attention in international literature and is now being imported to France and experimented with in a number of "inclusive" services, which combine different approaches to respond to the complexity of problems and the diversity of patients. In this approach, play and the therapeutic qualities of empathy and receptiveness are also key. The *3i* method, also based on individual play and the therapist's ability to create a relationship with the child, has had interesting results, which are soon to be published. Without speaking about a return to psychoanalysis, it seems clear that the methods which foreground interaction are increasingly more popular and valued. *Affinity Therapy*, which is also under evaluation, seems very promising. This method is based on the fact that knowledge (*savoir*) is located not only on the side of the caregiver, but also on the side of the autistic patients.

What can we expect from a psychoanalytic treatment of autistic children? These treatments, which generally require two or three sessions per week, have several different goals:

1   Starting from the hypothesis of the construction of and the progressive access to intersubjectivity, the analytic treatment with autists tries to make the child aware of the other's existence as non-threatening. There is a dialectic between subjectivisation and the access to intersubjectivity. The recognition of the other and of my self as a subject are part of the same movement. The goal is thus two-fold: that the subject sees himself as a subject, and as distinct from the other, with whom he can interact without too much danger.
2   Certain stereotypical behaviours and figurations can be given meaning by the analyst, making it possible to put words to what the child tries to represent or show to the other.
3   The emotions felt by the autistic child can also be identified using words. The analyst's role is to facilitate this process. Thanks to his empathy and his experience of transference and countertransference, the analyst is well placed to decode these messages.
4   The child thus has the experience of being able to communicate a part of his psychic life and experience to the other, without being destroyed in return.

5   Autistic children experience very archaic forms of anxiety, which manifest during psychoanalysis as well as in daily life. These are anxieties of being drained or emptied, of fragmentation or dissolution – hence the common search for solid means of support, for instance a wall to lean on. Faced with these moments of terror during the treatment, the analyst can put words to these archaic anxieties.

Autists experience strong and intense forms of mental distress and though I understand that in the case of some strongly behaviourist methods, a certain distancing from this suffering, from a methodological rather than epistemological perspective, is needed in order to take care of these patients, denying this suffering is unacceptable. Such denial is in itself a form of abuse and there are numerous testimonies of autists who have experienced some degree of it. For example, Temple Grandin (2006) or Michelle Dawson say very clearly that the forced use of purely behaviourist methods is a form of abuse and, while they do not explicitly rehabilitate psychoanalysis, they advocate the need to respect the autistic person, her desires, and her atypical development.

To conclude, it seems that, as it is often the case, we see a kind of pendulum movement in psychiatry: after the years of "psychoanalytic arrogance", when psychoanalysis claimed a hegemony and provided a metalanguage to preside over all other discourses, and following the subsequent era of "scientistic arrogance", which expected to soon discover the biological markers of all mental pathologies, we seem to be slowly returning to a more balanced situation, especially concerning autism.

Scientific triumphalism at the service of various commercial interests has now left room for doubt, especially regarding the long-term validity of the results of purely behaviourist methods (Shea, 2004; Mesibov & Shea, 2010). Some user groups have tried to use medical activism, lobbying, and PR to obtain what science has not provided. They have sometimes been able to influence policymakers, but the reality is clear: there is no scientific truth about autism, no possibility to diagnose autism based on biological markers, which obstructs prevention, and finally no method can claim to heal autism or even achieve very satisfying results.

In this context, psychodynamic and especially psychoanalytic methods remain relevant, on the condition of carefully establishing the indications, of choosing the right therapists, who require certain qualities, and combining these treatments with other educational or re-educational types of care. The psychoanalyst's boldest challenge is to suppose a subject in a being who does not speak, who does not seem to understand what is being said to him, who practically does not communicate through non-verbal means and often exhibits bewildering behaviour. Based on this supposition, psychoanalysts try to understand, using descriptive models, the psychic functioning, especially drive functioning, of the specific individual and adapt their practice to this supposed psychic reality. This method may seem insufficiently active, but, once again, it is never used as the only approach. At the same time, it is doubtful whether the long-term results of 100% active or hyper-active methods are in fact any better.

In 2017, autisms sadly remain just as opaque and mysterious. Faced with this inescapable fact, which leads to uncertainty, we must resist both the dogmatic and overly impassioned reactions. Psychoanalytic totalitarianism has failed, but behaviourist totalitarianism has failed as well.

References

American Psychiatric Association (2013). *Diagnostic and Statistical Manual of Mental Disorders* (5th ed.). Arlington, VA: American Psychiatric Publishing.

Bower, T. (1974). *Developent in Infancy*. San Francisco: Freeman.

Brazelton, T., Koslowski, B. & Main, M. (1974). The origins of reciprocity: the early mother-infant interaction. In M. Lewis and L. Rosenbum (Eds.), *The Effect of the Infant on its Caregiver*. New York: Wiley.

Freud, S. (1905). Three essays on the theory of sexuality. *Standard Edition* (Vol. 7, p. 123–246). London: Hogarth.

Golse, B. (2013). *Mon combat pour les enfants autistes*. Paris: Odile Jacob.

Grandin, T. (2006). *Thinking in Pictures: My Life with Autism*. New York: Vintage.

Hochmann, J. (1990). L'autisme infantile: déficit ou défense? In Ph.-J. Parquet, C. Bursztejn, & B. Golse (Eds.), *Soigner, éduquer l'enfant autiste?* Paris: Masson, p. 33–55.

Klein, M. (1946). Notes on some schizoid mechanisms. *International Journal of Psycho-Analysis*, 27, 99–110.

La Croix (2016). Autisme: Inserm recompense une chercheuse tourangelle [Autism: Inserm award goes to a Tours researcher]. 6 December 2016. Retrieved from: www.la-croix.com/Sciences/Autisme-Inserm-recompense-chercheuse-tourangelle-2016-12-06-1300808467 on 25 February 2018.

Meltzer, D. (1972). *Sexual States of Mind*. Paris: Payot.

Mesibov, G.B. & Shea, V. (2010). Evidence-based practice and autism. *Autism*, 15(1), 114–133.

Miller, J. (2013). *Closely Observed Infants*. London: Bloomsbury.

Mottron, L. (2016). *Intervention précoce pour les enfants autistes. Nouveaux principes pour soutenir une autre intelligence*. Ixelles: Mardaga.

Rey-Flaud, H. (2010). *L'enfant qui s'est arrêté au seuil du langage: Comprendre l'autisme*. Paris: Champs Essai.

Shea, V. (2004). A perspective on the research literature related to early intensive behavioral intervention (Lovaas) for young children with autism. *Autism*, 8(4), 349–367.

Thurin, J.-M., Thurin, M., Cohen, D. & Falissard, B. (2014). Approches psychothérapiques de l'autisme. Résultats préliminaires à partir de 50 études intensives de cas. *Neuropsychiatrie de l'Enfance et de l'Adolescence*, 62(2), 102–118.

Trevarthen, C. (1979). Communication and cooperation in early infancy: A description of primary intersubjectivity. In M. M. Bullowa (Ed.), *Before Speech: The Beginning of Interpersonal Communication*. New York: Cambridge University Press, 321–348.

Tustin, F. (1922). *Autistic States in Children*. London: Routledge.

Chapter 7

Diagnosing and educating autistic children today[1]

Iván Ruiz Acero and Neus Carbonell Camós

Javier's parents made an appointment for their son soon after he had turned two. Their paediatrician had noticed signs of withdrawal, a complete absence of speech and a degree of isolation from the Other. And indeed, in the first sessions the little boy exhibited certain signs of autism. We therefore decided to start working with Javier and his parents in a way that would enable us to diagnose his relational difficulties quickly and with more precision. Not long after, an element appeared that helped him tolerate staying in the sessions with a person he did not know: the action of counting "one, two, three!" and then throwing away a toy truck would immediately draw his attention and earn a little smile of satisfaction. His obvious interest and the smile for the other – traits already established in this little boy – contrasted strongly with a series of autistic signs that, not without reason, had alarmed the paediatrician. Another element had to be taken into account before tackling his actual difficulties: Javier's mother, conscious of the situation, had asked me not to rush to diagnose autism, while suggesting that in the meantime we describe Javier as having "special-needs". This initial stage would have normally led to a diagnosis, but in this case, we thought it was best not to come to any hasty conclusions.

However, the uncertainty around the development of young children such as this little boy often leads parents to consult a whole range of professionals. It is only at a later stage that they are able to place their trust in a specific clinician. Javier's parents thus decided to ask for a second opinion at a prestigious centre offering speedy diagnoses. The centre was not going to provide the treatment they believed was necessary, but, for a fee, would produce a diagnostic label to determine the child's situation.

After carrying out some of the most commonly used tests to diagnose autism spectrum disorder (on both Javier and his parents), experts from the centre decided on "autism spectrum disorder with a cognitive delay". In addition to this written diagnosis, they also said, when speaking to the parents: "This child will never be intelligent." Today, Javier speaks. He can turn towards the other to ask a question or complain, to play and laugh. Now aged four, he can count – one, two, three... and much further – and is able to

DOI: 10.4324/9781003221487-8

read and write. His initial autism has been reduced to a degree of fixation in relating to others. There is nothing left of the fatal prognosis produced by the tests. These could not have predicted the importance of the need for an openness to the Other, which was there at the very beginning, or the value of the signifier "special-needs", by which especially Javier's mother effectively designated her son as an unclassifiable human being.

Diagnosis of autistic symptoms

As psychoanalysts, we understand diagnosis as the detection of symptoms that affect and profoundly involve the human subject. However, there is a great difference between diagnosing the difficulties presented by a subject and finding a "label" that claims to define and name his being. Today's concern with naming the subject's being using a pathological diagnosis – as depressed, hyperactive, or an addict – has an even greater effect in the case of autism, given that its spectrum continues to widen, slowly becoming a general category that also includes symptoms not strictly speaking autistic.

The website on "autisms",[2] created by the Fundación del Campo Freudiano, defines autism using the plural "autisms", as a

> particular form of situating oneself in the world and constructing a reality for oneself. Associated or not with organic causes, autism is recognisable by its symptoms, which impede or severely restrict a child's entrance into language, communication and the social link. Stereotypies, echolalia, absence of language, soliloquies, self-aggression, insensitivity to pain or lack of fear of danger are all symptoms that express a child's or adult's isolation from the world that surrounds them and a tendency towards self-sufficiency.

Rather than considering autism an illness, for which we would need to find a unique and chronic causal agent, psychoanalysis instead approaches it as a position, at times extreme, that a subject may take towards his body, objects and the Other. This hypothesis aligns with Jacques Lacan's understanding of a subject's original condition. In the human being, he claimed, not everything can pass through the filter of language. In other words, we cannot inscribe ourselves in the world without the experience of what remains outside this inscription.

Diagnosing autism in early infancy does therefore not mean simply isolating the symptoms making a child or his parents suffer. Nor does it consist solely in highlighting a developmental abnormality. It means, above all, understanding, as much as possible, that in some distant time and place the subject made a kind of decision while trying to defend himself from anxiety. His modes of dealing with his body, of choosing his own objects, and maintaining a liveable distance between himself and others will be correlated to this position, adopted in the face of anguish.

At present, diagnostic manuals stick to fixed descriptions of observable elements predefined by the very same manual. What is diagnosed is what can be seen, reducing human beings to their behaviour. A repetitive hand movement spinning an object is considered a stereotype, just like the same movement made by a child hoping an adult will hand him a cookie. Hand movements are clearly observable and when they seem repetitive, they become "stereotypies". In addition, behaviours are – quite mistakenly – seen as being measurable in terms of duration and frequency, without any need to pay attention to the specific function they may hold in the given context.

Today, the most commonly used tests to diagnose autism spectrum disorder are based on the countability of observable behaviours, to determine if they fall within the normal range of what is expected from a child of a certain age. These test results have no means of accounting for the meaning of each behaviour for that particular child; it is deemed normal or pathological from the standpoint of the observing adult, rather than the child. When applied to the child in the presence of his parents, the situations staged by these tests can often be rather absurd, to say the least.

Hector's parents attend his first appointment with a psychologist, who tells them she needs to do a general development assessment. She asks them to give Hector a book, in order to see "how the boy handles it". Hector likes books; to him, they are objects of great potential. He takes the book and puts it to his ear to see if it perhaps makes music; he opens it to listen to the creaking of the spine and runs his fingers through it, producing the sound typically made by friction on a solid surface. The psychologist contemplates the options in the test and concludes that "the child cannot handle the book".

True, at the age of two, Hector does not inspect the book in order to enjoy its drawings, to point to a figure and say "mummy" or be entertained by going through its pages one by one. He does not interact with the book in a "standard" way, but rather as if it is an object that can be enjoyed beyond its expected purpose. Why cannot a non-standard use of an object like this fit the criteria of this or another test? In reality, adults are expected to make novel use of many different objects. Are there no adults who treat books as if they were just objects, enjoying them for their visual presentation, size, smell, or simply to fill their shelves?

Diagnostic caution

There is no doubt that the diagnosis of mental disorders is a complicated field. It is not by accident that the current plethora of tests – whether they replace or complement one another and are adjusted to the child's age – seek to establish a consensus about what constitutes autism today. However, problems arise if we forget that such a diagnosis can become a double-edged sword. Even with our best intentions, a diagnosis may have severe segregation effects.

A diagnosis of autism is normally received by the parents as either arriving too early or too late, no matter how many protocols have been used. Why isn't there a "right" moment to accept this diagnostic label? Simply because the naming produced by a diagnosis relegates the subject to a general category. Its immediate effect is to subsume the adjectives previously describing the child under a generality, while leaving the particularities of each subject unrepresented.

Some adults have referred to the conflict between the received diagnosis and the words they themselves use to describe their experience. Albert, one of the protagonists of the documentary *Otras Voces. Una Mirada Diferente Sobre el Autismo* ("Other Voices: A Different Perspective on Autism"), could not express this better: "Of course, everyone has their oddities, but the way I describe them makes them more attractive to me. And that's the most interesting part: not everything is Asperger's – I also have my personality."

Consensus on diagnostic signs

Many of the most common symptoms of autism are diagnostic indices on which there is clear-enough consensus among clinicians, including those having the most contrary conceptions of autism. The list is long; its elements broadly refer to the following three levels: the subjectivisation of one's own body, the relation with objects, and the bond with the Other. The *autistic spectrum disorder* remains a clinical diagnosis, which means that the diagnostic procedure consists in observing the subject over time and with respect to these three dimensions. The reason is that in terms of the physiological basis of autism, the results of the tests now considered part of the protocol have so far not been considered diagnostically conclusive.

Autism: a magnifying glass on humanity

However, a general consensus on what should be observed does not mean there is a shared interpretation of what is happening. And even if such interpretation existed, it would not necessarily help us detect the important difficulties in a child's life, but might instead simply justify them from a common sense perspective, especially during infancy. What difference could there be between an "absence of language" and "shyness" in a child? Or between "expressions of anxiety" when an object is taken away and "strong character"? This eagerness to understand a child's symptom by what can be explained as simply part of childhood – shyness, defiance, being nervous, or "doing things one's own way", etc. – often serves the desire *not to know* what is actually going on. We often hear parents describe a moment like this, where the effort *not to see* overrides the evidence.

If autistic symptoms can be explained away by this kind of common sense, it is because at the very heart of this condition we find the clearest manifestations of what it is to be human. A rejection of the expressiveness of the gaze and the voice, repetitive actions, rigid rituals that accompany daily life, a difficulty accessing intimacy, a need to "disconnect from the world" or even stereotypies are subjective signs that autism makes patently visible, as if under a giant magnifying glass. But isn't the repetitive movement of crossing one leg over the other in an adult also a stereotype, one with a very specific tranquilising function?

Be that as it may, the often radical rejection of the difficulties posed by autism could be seen as a very human reaction, especially when dealing with an *infans* with whom a bond is yet to be constructed. Hence, the diagnosis cannot be presented as a direct confrontation with the initial desire *not to know* that is likely to manifest in the adult. The moment of diagnosing the child's difficulties must respect the time needed by his parents.

Autism for all?

We live in an era with a penchant for classification and a tendency to police all variations from the norm. Over the recent decades, the Diagnostic and Statistical Manual of Mental Disorders (DSM) elaborated by the American Psychiatric Association (APA) has managed to erase from the global mental health map some of the crucial findings of 19th-century and early 20th-century psychiatry. These foregrounded the concept of human subjectivity; they established nosographic categories by observing the pathological symptoms and listening to what patients had to say about their own suffering. The type of psychiatry based on studying what happens to a subject when he is with others began to be dismantled during the mid-1970s, the field instead turning towards more biological perspectives and finally transforming into a discipline focused on the organism. Starting with DSM-III, the aim was to produce a classification that could be applied more effectively, modifying those categories that were considered obsolete after only a few years and replacing them with others, better adapted to today's symptomatology. These classifications cover practically all of the symptoms human beings present just by virtue of being alive and living with others, thus giving free rein to pharmaceutical companies keen to offer the most suitable drugs.

We find ourselves at the convergence of capitalist discourse, which has raised medication to the level of a commodity, with health administrations worshipping what Éric Laurent has called "the ideal of a generally medicalised existence". The situation became so extreme that a global "Stop DSM" mobilisation, together with other protests and enquiries – including from within the APA itself – were able to delay the manual's new edition. There was even a petition, by one of the sectors of American psychiatry, calling on the World Health Organization to intervene.

The ethical debate this issue raises is directly related to our approaches to autism. Over the last 20 years, the number of the items listed as part of the *autism spectrum disorder* has grown ten-fold. In the next edition, it is expected its limits will further expand, to include, for example, the so-called Asperger syndrome, as well as many other language disorders not previously associated with this diagnosis.

This has in fact already happened in the case of the *attention deficit hyperactivity disorder* (ADHD), which has proliferated among the child population, converting many problems typical of childhood into a pathology. Today, it in fact also concerns a great many adults, who were supposedly formerly undiagnosed hyperactive children. The *autism spectrum disorder* (ASD) is currently following the same trend, becoming a kind of *ready-made* diagnosis applicable to any stage in a child's life that may accentuate some of the spectrum's extremes: from relational and communication problems to affective and mood disorders. And, just like in the case of ADHD, where the diagnosis was launched simultaneously with the drugs supposed to treat it, there is likely going to be the same pharmaceutical response to the ASD diagnosis, disseminated due to its multiple symptoms. And who could oppose someone's right to suffer from ASD, once there is a drug expected to treat it?

The current prominence of autism in social and healthcare policies – France declared it the "Great National Cause for 2012" – enables us to review both the theory and practice related to this highly complex subject. At the same time, it highlights a reality that was previously kept under wraps. However, social advances are never without effects: the generalisation of autism has resulted in a strange, poorly defined spectrum, one that leads to diagnostic errors and often has irreparable consequences for both subjects and their families. For many clinicians, who are forced to provide speedy diagnoses – and follow treatment protocols – this sense of disorientation creates a great deal of anxiety. All of this goes hand in hand with an impoverishment of the clinic and a growing sense of alarm among the public, which drives politicians to enact laws in haste, thus simplifying a complex reality in an effort at more effective legislation.

The dignity of each subject

The diagnosis of autism requires a pre-existing hypothesis about what is happening, and therefore also a proposition of treatment. If the hypothesis is that of a neurophysiological disorder due to which autists fail to correctly learn certain social behaviours, then all the non-standard behaviours shown by an autistic child must be rectified. Re-education methods that proliferate today seek to remove these "incorrectly learnt behaviours", making the child adopt more suitable behaviours at any cost. Hence the surprise felt by parents when clinicians ask them to eradicate stereotypies, if necessary, through "negative reinforcement" (a behaviourist euphemism for punishment). The argument is that these behaviours are useless and antisocial. Who will consider the parents' question about the possible function these stereotypies might have for their child? If the etiological hypothesis is a neurophysiological disorder, such questions become irrelevant: it is the brain and not the child that matters.

On the contrary, when the initial hypothesis is that in the so-called autistic child there is a subject, one who has adopted a radical stance towards the outside world as a stable protection measure against anxiety, his behaviours – even if impeded by a real neurophysiological condition – can be interpreted and contemplated as properly human. Consequently, the treatment proposed by psychoanalysis continues to defend a perspective which reaffirms the autist's status as a subject and confers to his world all its dignity.

Notes

1 This text is an abridged version of two chapters ("Cómo se diagnostica el autismo?" and "Educación y autismo") originally published in Ruiz Acero & Carbonell Camós (2013), *No todo sobre el autismo*. Barcelona: RBA Libros.
2 Unfortunately, the website www.autismos.es, created by the Barcelona Clinical Section of the Foundation of the Freudian Field (today part of the World Association of Psychoanalysis), is no longer available.

Chapter 8

Autism

The French debate

Pierre-Henri Castel

In France, the treatment of autism has been the topic of significant controversy, the epistemological aspects of which are directly connected to its sociological dimension. The violence of these debates, or at least the way they have been framed by their key actors, has to do with the fierceness of the following opposition. On the one hand, we have university psychiatrists and psychologists of behaviourist orientation who are united in the field of international research (yet absolutely not the leading researchers known to the general public) and are scandalised – not too strong a word – by the anomalous persistence, in France, of "more or less psychoanalytic" (or psychodynamic) treatments of autists, whom they prefer to refer to, using the current terminology, as suffering from "pervasive developmental disorders". Following a mechanism familiar to the sociology of medicine, their demands for the complete eradication of psychoanalysis from the treatment of autism are supported by parent groups, which call upon them as experts, at times contrary to the caregivers. For a long time, their anger was fuelled in particular by one supposedly therapeutic method, of which there exist many different and detailed psychoanalytic justifications: what is in France known as *packing*, i.e. the method of therapeutic envelopment using wet sheets. It consists in wrapping the patient – usually an extremely agitated autist – in towels that are slowly soaked in lukewarm water. Their tightening provides a gradual form of containment and allegedly an appeasement. This strategy was implemented to replace tranquilliser shots, because French child psychiatry has been very resistant to the use of powerful drugs in the treatment of children. Packing has been violently criticised and even described as a form of torture; the French delay in implementing "methods that work" (ABA, TEACCH, etc.) has even been denounced in the French Parliament.

On the other hand, there is the large community of psychiatrists who only rarely work in the university hospital services and are instead employed by the many public or semi-public institutions functioning throughout France and caring for all sorts of children with mental difficulties, as well as the psychologists-psychoanalysts working in these institutions, and finally the psychoanalysts in private practice. They too are outraged, but by the theories and practices of their adversaries, whom they, again, shower with accusations:

DOI: 10.4324/9781003221487-9

of overestimating their scientific notions of autism and, unable to offer anything better, selling a kind of "animal training" procedures dressed up in scientistic justifications, which not only cannot cure autism (understood as an incurable neurobiological condition) but also have no respect for the "subjectivity" of their patients.

However, in recent years we have witnessed a striking phenomenon. For many years, parent support groups would only voice complaints about the conventional forms of treatment, which in the French public health sector were inevitably marked by psychoanalysis. (And many biographical research studies of families have shown and documented that blaming mothers was and remains a common, and obviously very badly perceived, response in these types of care.) However, over the last decade, we have seen the rising influence of parents' groups that are very much attached to the forms of care marked by psychoanalysis and who refuse using the methods they too consider a mere form of "training". They emphasise the family's right to a free choice of a therapist, especially when the latter commits to long-term and highly personalised work. The ability of these groups to make their voices heard is of course by far lesser than those violently opposed to psychoanalysis – but neither it is negligible and it has had a certain influence on the political and administrative structures which, in France, both locally and nationally, control the healthcare system. Indeed, it is difficult to reject – even in the name of science or the international consensus on "methods that work" – the voices that call for the respect of individual freedom, of the free choice of therapists and the autonomy of families in terms of the types of care they want for their children. To complicate things further, in a number of ongoing trials it has transpired that the behaviourist treatments much vaunted for a specific category of "receptive" autists could easily result in clearly abusive practices. If the enemies of psychoanalysis have *packing*, the opponents of these behaviourist methods now speak about cases of "less receptive" children who have been restrained and even beaten by exhausted therapists.

This is to say that autism has become the nerve centre of what Alain Ehrenberg has called the "wars of the subject" in France, essentially a value conflict proper to the style of individualism exercised in my home country. The latter systematically stages a struggle between, on the one hand, representations of autonomy that are rationalist but also technocratic, normatively centralised under the control of the State, and validated by its institutions and, on the other hand, private freedoms, a certain right to exception, which *also* requires public support, especially financial support. Thus we are witnessing a rare spectacle of learned actors contesting the scientific validity of the other camp's arguments, but rather than in scholarly journals or behind the walls of academic establishments (because each camp has their own), they are doing so *in the public square*, while calling on public opinion. The goal is to win the State over to one's side: either to legally obtain the definitive eradication of the plague of psychoanalysis, that anti-scientific aberration, or to defend the inalienable right of families and individuals to desire a personal and subjective destiny for beings suffering from a mysterious condition, which nonetheless has the flavour of a family tragedy. Petitions and counter-petitions on autism (and, by the way, many other children's mental disorders) are thus part of the French folklore, to the bafflement of foreign scholars.

Even the way these camps see one another is striking. It never occurs to them that the reasons for their dispute might have more to do with the moral and political configurations of the questions of the individual and society *in France*. To them, these are *universal* considerations about science or ethics – never institutional configurations, their history, nor the entire series of other political, judicial, economic, sociological, and other contradictions in which these institutions are caught up and which explain the violence of this debate. There are simply good and bad practices and the inexpiable war of a "clinic of the subject" (yum!) against a "clinic of the brain and behaviour" (yuck!), or the war of authentic scientists against self-serving charlatans. One side believes that the very survival of psychoanalysis is an unfortunate French cultural artefact, related to the well-known predilection for gibberish and elitist pretentions this side of the Channel. To the other side, the unbearable claims of neuroscientists and behaviourists of being able to dictate what is good practice in terms of treating autism is evidence of the growing medicalisation of the human condition, or even of neoliberal dehumanisation.

I am only giving you a rough outline of the situation, and if it seems caricatural to some readers, it is because it is indeed full of caricatures. I will thus begin by using the tools of social anthropology to introduce some *distanciation*, to describe the many difficulties and contingencies affecting those working with autists in France, regardless of whether they defend the *objective* neuroscientific and behaviourist approaches or turn toward a *social* psychiatry strongly marked by psychoanalysis. To conclude, I will defend the *politically engaged* idea that the impasse of the French debate has to do especially with psychoanalysts, in their large majority, trying to support an indefensible "psychoanalytic psychopathology" of autism that would counter term by term the new neuroscientific and behaviourist theories. However, my main point is not that this psychopathology is ridiculous. Rather, this intellectualist ideology, which imitates the more or less outdated forms of scientificity, *obscures* the genuine understanding that these "clinicians of the subject" have of the social reality that autism *also* represents – not only in terms of the individual conditions of specific families, but also the larger social ideals and normative expectations, as well as the more or less unbearable pressure exerted on us in their name. Because it cannot situate itself as part of a determined social and historical process, and even claims a kind of transcendence vis-à-vis the political and social field, French psychoanalysis of autism only helps feed the monsters of abstraction, while its useless anxiety prevents it from recognising the principles of its true relevance and its *relative* security in the contemporary social landscape.

One might believe that such a burning mental health issue, so specifically French and with so many larger resonances, would have been a magnet for anthropologists. And yet this is not the case. Very few empirical, ethnographic, and sociological studies have examined our institutions looking after autistic children – these split, conflict-ridden establishments, full of practitioners adhering to different models yet committed to working together in public service. Studying them is a delicate matter, not only because of the difficult access to the field (the suspicious attitude of medical teams, the question of minors, etc.), but also because they cannot stop at drawing a distant social portrait of the families and caregivers or clarifying the possible care paths and their bifurcations (in some circumstances taking the psychoanalytic route, in others following the behaviourist orientation). They also have to go deeper into the details of these practices, using ethnographic tools to examine, for example, how diagnoses are scientifically justified by tests, i.e. by what the actors consider to be the least socially biased, most objective, or most natural (the key moment in which the brain unveils itself and the rest becomes mere chatter). However, a project of this kind requires the anthropologist to have a solid command of not just neuroscience but also all of the philosophies of mind, action, and intentionality that are its rational underpinnings. Herein lies the value of the long and rigorous research carried out by Céline Borelle and published three years ago as *Diagnosing Autism: A Sociological Approach* (Borelle, 2017). As we might have expected, because this work comes from outside the field of the controversy and instead tries to reconstruct the foundations of the practices concerned, neither of the two camps has taken notice of its existence.

The strength of the book is that it focuses its inquiry on the contentious status of the ideas of autonomy and the process of *empowerment* (*autonomisation*), which are obviously inhibited among the so-called "autists". It then maps out the raging conflict about what this autonomy might mean. Can it be naturalised, i.e. understood exclusively as a matter of *individual cognitive functioning*, rooted in the brain and the genetic makeup of the individuals in question? Or is there something about autism that is *irreducibly relational* (which does not necessarily mean that the psychoanalytic view of this relationship should be prioritised)? However, the battlefield of autism always affects many others, primarily because it is related to the medical institutions working in mental health, to questions of family and childhood, to the activism of self-help groups, the public healthcare policies, and even to human rights (the idea of the dignity of each "person" or "subject"), to the scientific and academic status of psychology (extremely different from what is called psychology in the United Kingdom), and so on. In this sense, Borelle paints a moral portrait of our divisions, of the French cultural "discontents", faced with a terrible impasse of empowerment of children. And she rightly shows that the seemingly dominant debate between the scientific-objective and ethical-subjective visions of autism is in fact *subordinate* to it.

She immediately puts her finger on the painful question of diagnosis. In the French debate and to the great surprise of foreign observers, the positive refusal to diagnose autism in a certain tradition of social child psychiatry and psychoanalysis has been met with furious opposition from behaviourists and neuroscientists. The latter see it as an obstacle to accessing standardised care, a form of obscurantist denial of the reality of the illness (which is treated as relational or psychological or – how outrageous – Oedipal!) and in any case (which is highly relevant in our healthcare system) as an irresponsible delay in accessing the social support to which the parents and children are entitled.

In other words, the question of diagnosis concentrates the entirety of this debate and Borelle shows very clearly that all the different strands develop from this central point. Her research was therefore carried out between two institutions. One of them looks after children with all kinds of problems. Its psychologists and psychiatrists, with a social conscience and often very inspired, if not trained, by psychoanalysis, express a suspiciousness towards the notion of autism, while observing children *in their family*. The other, a specialised diagnostic centre charged with separating "true" autists from those that merely resemble them or those simply unrelated to and excluded from this field of medico-social care, is populated by psychiatrists and psychologists who do not actually treat children or support families, but who have been trained in the use of objective methods. How do these two institutions communicate with each other; what are the moral stakes of diagnosis; what are its social effects, not just on the diagnosed children but their parents and caregivers? We see immediately that the problem is *absolutely not epistemological*. Those who resort to epistemology only do so in order to *socially* overpower their adversaries in the name of certain norms and values.

Hence the importance, when we speak about autism, of putting "diagnosis" in quotation marks. There is already the fact that this is a *diagnosis without a care prescription*, because, as we are told, autism is an incurable neurodevelopmental disorder. However, even if it was a developmental disorder, it is also a diagnosis *without a clear prognosis*. We can more or less extend the neurocognitive developmental curves, but we cannot predict how an autistic child is going to "develop", in other words, his possibility of suddenly accessing a higher level of cognitive and thus social performance. And as Borelle points out, not only in theory but also in the concrete practice of treatments she has observed in her specialised centre, a child diagnosed as "autistic" but who has "evolved" in this qualitative sense leaves the category of autism behind. However, the variety of care paths and even the cognitive and social plasticity of individuals diagnosed as "autistic" (or seemingly autistic) is considerable. "Diagnosis" (in quotation marks), also because it is not based on *any etiopathogenesis* (there is still not even the tiniest constant biological marker for this condition, just a bunch of clusters of all kinds of indexes with hardly any overlap between them).

So, what remains? A highly formalised diagnostic *technique* based on tests, which tries to introduce a minimum of standardisation into heterogenous situations. Borelle describes the *Autism Diagnostic Interview* (ADI) and *Autism Diagnostic Observation Schedule* (ADOS), implemented and included in the work of the specialised centre of her ethnographic study. We should be careful not to let the detailed descriptions of the protocols observed simply make us feel uncomfortable as to the objectivity of the results. It is already something that we can actually arrive at a *relative* descriptive stability and that clinicians can agree among themselves on diagnostic inclusion and exclusion. The key point is rather that the autistic disorder appears initially in a relational, intra-familiar context, at school, etc. In other words, clinicians and parents have a strong and above all *prior* intuition of whether a child is autistic or not. And this intuition has been formed upstream, especially in the institution that refers children to the specialised centre. The formalised tests then appear as a way of refining this intuitive judgement and, most importantly, *aligning* the clinical picture with a pre-constructed medico-social category that gives access to welfare rights, for example to specialised education and benefits, without any certainty that an objective pathological entity has been identified. In reality, these highly standardised tests could very well be revised (they serve above all as tools of standardisation), with considerable legal and medico-social consequences for the people who are treated on their basis. (This is what has happened in the United States, where some of the "high-functioning" or Asperger autists have seen their institutional aid withdrawn.) At the same time, in order for them to be operational, the risk of these assessments being seen as purely a matter of convention has to be eliminated. We must therefore continuously strive to *naturalise* these disorders, turning them into the expression of something = x that happens in the child's head (in his brain), without ever having obtained the tiniest evidence to support this hypothesis.

Because Borelle describes practice rather than just theory, we now understand the constant references to a "functional" disorder, in order to individualise and, crucially, localise *in the brain* the manifestation of impairments, which, as nobody contests, manifest above all *in relational systems* (family, school, etc.). However, once again, this is not a kind of pseudo-objectivity. It is not an error and much less a scientistic deception, but rather a strong compulsion linked to the very construction of the system of tests and its *use* by families and care institutions, protected by our values of solidarity with people in need.

Simply put, Borelle argues, intuition is everywhere and scientific judgement with its naturalising tendencies always comes *as a supplement* to it. Her ethnographic study highlights all the instances of intuition in the different and often silent practices, which are only occasionally justified by resorting to formal medical categories. There is the intuition of the secretary who picks up the phone and functions as the first gatekeeper, de facto diagnosing the *legitimacy* of the demand for diagnosis. Then, the parents often have fairly accurate intuitions about the kinds of problems their child is suffering from. However, Borelle shows, they have an incentive to *conceal* the true extent of their understanding before those who remain the "masters" of diagnosis and thus the "arbiters" of the child's medico-social destiny. Incidentally, she thus confirms something that is very difficult for professionals to endorse: year after year, the long elaboration of the child's difficulties that the parents have already experienced, the information gleaned on the Internet, all contribute to the fact that the announcement of the diagnosis is precisely *not as traumatic* as it is often described in psychoanalytic literature. Often, it is even a relief. It means entering a new phase where it is at last *possible to act*, as all of the parents who reclaim their right to diagnosis continue to repeat. Thus, an opportunity for empowerment.

Borelle also presents the two main arguments of the adversaries of this "right to diagnosis", so hotly contested in France, in other words of those who prefer leaving things open, following a "psychodynamic" (psychoanalytical) perspective. On the one hand, there is the familiar experience that many children will unexpectedly undergo a qualitative development. Many will therefore not correspond to the clinical pictures characterised by various deficits that still tend to dominate the medical expectations in the field of autism. On the other hand, those most adverse to the right to diagnosis are often the heirs of antipsychiatry, who believe that it is morally if not politically reprehensible to confine anyone to a diagnostic category that could result in a permanent stigma. However, the series of intuitions does not stop here. There is also the fact, as Borelle shows, that the diagnostic process has to be supported by a "genuine demand" of the parents, or even children (to the extent that if a teenager wants to interrupt their process of diagnosis, they have a right to do so, one head physician argues). This "genuine demand" must be a proof of a relational distress between the parents and the child that is both authentic and decipherable, even though this *relational* distress will ultimately be recoded as a *functional* distress located in the brain of the suffering individual, because autonomy must be respected across the board. Yet how do we identify a "genuine demand"? Lastly, the ultimate space ruled by intuition: having left the centre with a "diagnosis", one is left without treatment, without prognosis, without any cause of the ailment. There are only the practices I would describe as ortho-pedagogical, which favour the *social idea* that parents, doctors, and social workers have of the child's process of empowerment – a social idea that is precisely not a critical sociological concept but remains more or less akin to intuition, if not prejudice.

Finally, what gives the term "diagnosis" of autism its special flavour is not only that it is imbued with formal conventions that are more scientistic than scientific. It has been pared down so as to *a priori* exclude a relational causality that could play into a psychoanalytic reading. There are indeed situations where one is tempted to see the school and family environment as having played a direct role in the formation of the symptoms. These are the so-called *autistic-like* symptoms sometimes observed in orphanages, but also in major cases of "emotional deprivation" experienced by young children, to employ the terminology used by our institutions. Professionals agree that in these cases the external envelope of the symptom is near-identical to that of autism properly speaking. *Unaware of this context*, we could in fact not distinguish between "genuine" autists and *autistic-like* children based on observable information alone (and even standardised tests, without taking relational factors into account, would result in too many positives). However, once we know about this generally intra-familial context, it is no longer autism. This exclusion process therefore disqualifies, from the outset, situations that would have once led psychoanalysts to make excessive generalisations about the psychogenic and family origins of autism. And yet, as the study shows, these cases are far from rare. Of course, this does not at all mean that the psychogenic theories are correct. They are notoriously unable to account for those cases of autism that cannot be explained by the context. However, it is noteworthy that in reality uncertainties persist and the actors have a strong tendency to place front and centre what was previously on the margins, in order to outdo those who had confined to the margins what is now at the centre. This indicates that a *purely intellectual discussion* of autism will not suffice, as long as the norms, values, expectations and obligations of the different actors remain unclarified, with all their constraints but also the possibilities of action they offer to the respective sides. This is true for both psychoanalysis and the so-called objective approaches.

However, the truth is that we can never eliminate the relational dimension from the description of a child's "functional" disorder. Observing the different practices, Borelle also points out that when children are being tested, parents are questioned as to whether their child normally behaves in the same way he does during the test. The test is so *artificial* that we can never really know whether it unequivocally captures a disturbance of *ordinary* interaction. Is this anything but, once again, trusting the intuition of those related to the child inside his family (an intuition that is, by definition, never tested)?

There is thus an *ineliminable residual uncertainty* in the practical paradoxes encountered by the actors, but also in their clever ways of trying to unblock the situation and find coherent possibilities of action. Showing this is the most precious element of Borelle's analysis. Of course, the term "diagnosis" necessarily makes us uncomfortable, when it simply means an attempt to formalise, in hindsight, the shifting borders of an enigmatic abnormality, both in terms of its cause and its actual manifestations, its relational or substantial structure and its future development. However, the soundness of her comments lies in her highlighting the art of finding socially (and morally) acceptable solutions in situations of uncertainty. At times, these include actions that, seen from the outside, only appear as violations of a scientifically rigorous protocol or a cat-and-mouse game between unequal players.

What is certain is that in the case of autism there is no simple linearity between the discovery of the problematic situation, the diagnosis and its practical, medical, or other consequences. Rather we seem to be faced with an entire tree of possible choices, each of them likely to push the children and their families in a very different direction, where the very meaning of the word "autism" and the responsibilities related to it for both care teams and parents are constantly at risk of diverging. In other words, it is not a case of error versus truth. It would also be false to imagine that the space where these divergences abound is simply poorly organised. It is rather the opposite. The rigidly ordered series of trade-offs exist on both the psychodynamic and the more cognitivist-behaviourist side. The second fact that emerges from this study, and I wonder if it will be confirmed by others, is that you cannot strictly speaking say that the diagnosis of autism is a simple operation of *selection*. Selection is undoubtedly part of it, but operates within a hierarchy of diagnoses, with "typical" autism with all the rights and treatment possibilities it offers at its peak, followed by a gradient of less distinguished categories (pervasive developmental disorder – "not otherwise specified", a simple "intellectual disability", "emotional deprivation", and other autism-*like* syndromes). Their negotiation is not rooted in any undisputable objective referent, but instead mobilises family strategies, medical ideologies, and, finally, the social and moral values that lie at the centre of a debate constitutive of modern individualist societies: what does it mean to be "truly" autonomous? And if we cannot attain true autonomy, how can we at least come close to it?

It is therefore as if the debate between behaviourism and psychoanalysis concerned not so much the right theory of autism but the "right kind of autonomy". Behaviourists highlight action and thus the acquisition of social skills for both children and families. Psychoanalysts put more emphasis on meaning and affect, and hence on the emergence of a kind of subjective authenticity (even though they value its joint emergence in both children *and* their parents, who are encouraged to themselves undergo therapy). Behaviourists subscribe to an "activist" paradigm of autonomy, where, according to Borelle's formulation, the latter means *becoming responsible for* (*responsable "pour"*): for one's actions, for one's change, for putting oneself in question. In the autistic child, this approach is thus trying to facilitate the emergence of a *socially acceptable equivalent of ordinary intentionality*, obtained by tackling his difficulties head-on. In order to fight against stereotypies and repetitive movements characteristic of the behaviour of certain autists, a behaviourist psychologist suggests "repeating to death" in order to break the disabling habit (perhaps a neurologically based automatism) by acquiring an enabling counter-habit. You cannot obtain true autonomy or anything close to it without forcing empowerment against all odds. The partisans of a psychodynamic approach (the psychoanalysts) evoke a paradigm of autonomy which could be described as "ontological" rather than "activist" and which terrifies their adversaries: a *responsibility for* (*responsable "de"*) what one is, a responsibility for the meaning given to or deciphered from the events. However, this second type of responsibility presents a risk: it easily degenerates into guilt. In the psychoanalytic perspective, the ultimate responsibility is thus to enable the emergence (and definitely not by forcing anything) in the autistic child of an autonomous subjective intentionality, despite the severity of behavioural symptoms. In this view, the forced empowerment pursued by behaviourism, in other words, an illusion of autonomy obtained by "training", would be contrary to a genuine autonomy – one that is subjectively meaningful.

The point of this symmetrical depiction of the systems of values is that it provides an explanatory background to another key contribution of Borelle's work, which has to do with the notion of guilt. It has long been argued that the scandal of the psychoanalytic approach to autism lies in its tendency to "blame the mother". However, you only need to read the comments of the parents, slapped with the injunction to sort themselves out so they can properly take care of their kids, when it is no longer coming from the psychoanalytic field but from behaviourism, to see that blame has simply changed camps – but *continues to be directed at mothers*. The difference is that the latter are no longer ontologically at fault, à la Bettelheim, but instead shamefully lazy and unimaginative, in short, in the normative noose that behaviourist treatments tighten around their neck, they are simply seen as "incompetent". There is something just as infantilising in the criticisms addressed to them by behaviourists. However, to remedy this lack, mothers are no longer asked to convert by going deep into themselves and examining themselves on the couch, but to find support and stimulation (especially in the voluntary and community sector) to continue on what they all eloquently call their "obstacle course". Hence a displacement rather than an elimination of guilt.

After distanciation, Borell's work opens up new prospects for our involvement, especially as psychoanalysts. Once we no longer see the diverging views on autism as an *intellectual* conflict between truth and error, but rather as the ingenious practices of actors confronted with something quite uncertain or even impossible, but which still requires action and a constant search for more autonomy, we have a better idea of why these actors may be irresistibly attracted to purely psychological or, on the contrary, neurobiological conceptions of autism. Thus, defending a "psychoanalytic psychopathology" of autism with (highly) hypothetical empirical foundations is *precisely not* standing up for a relational approach; instead, it means adopting a naturalising but *Freudian* understanding of autism. It means giving the clinic of transference a function analogous to the diagnostic tests – and even going a bit further, because psychoanalytic psychopathology claims to understand the etiopathogenesis of the disorder. All of this we can do without. Because in order to authentically hold a relational position, it is not enough to emphasise the psychological factors. I wish to conclude with this point, which I hope will disappoint those psychoanalysts who imagine they know something both objective and specific about autism. None of their theories, no matter how brilliant or well-referenced, will be meaningful and morally and socially acceptable unless, rather than a theory of autism itself, they offer a theory of *what to do with* autism.

Because the great contribution of Borelle's approach, part of the so-called pragmatic sociology, is that she shows all that is *on the outside* in autism, the entire *social* network of relationships that transforms the nodes of "mother", "father", "child", etc. into correlated sites of distress, within a complex life form that has its own economic and statutory inequalities, its rational or moral norms, etc. Each degree of freedom gained in this direction is what gives any psychoanalytic concept or act its seriousness. And, to my mind, any psychoanalytic speculation that does not let itself be operationalised in terms of these degrees of freedom and does not retranslate itself into a better "doing with" autism (for the individual in question, his family, group, and even the entire society) is hollow.

References

Borelle, C. (2017). *Diagnostiquer l'autisme: Une approche sociologique*. Paris: Transvalor, Presses des mines.

Chapter 9

High-functioning autism and the ideology of behaviorism

Yann Diener

Freud, with his typical modesty, once said that writers were always far in advance of the discoveries of psychoanalysis. We see evidence of this every day. For instance, the writer François Meyronnis describes how, as a school child, his refusal to learn how to read and count bothered not just his teachers and parents but also his classmates. In his recent autobiography, Meyronnis writes: "[My teachers] did not know the way a single letter agitated a space and made it vibrate. How, thick with sound, it haunted the space and made it spin around, risking a spike here, a hook there" (Meyronnis, 2012, p. 12–13). When, as a child, he did not join in group games, when he would withdraw, his classmates would call him odd, only to then immediately deny him this status: "You pretend you're original, but deep down you're just like us." He would try to "bear witness to what cannot be measured". As an adult, he then endeavoured to "eliminate all ordinary measures". This could be taken as the very definition of topology, the branch of mathematics interested precisely in the relationships between elements rather than their measured distances.

Meyronnis describes how one evening, as a child, he became completely disoriented, not knowing in which direction he should face in his bed.

> Suddenly all spatial references went missing. A terrifying discovery of a hole in being, where up and down, right and left, all directions and azimuths had collapsed. ... As if I'd fallen through the cracks and into a vortex. The hole then spat me out again, and I found myself on the other side.
>
> (ibid., p. 17–18)

The psychoanalyst Donald Meltzer suggested that all autists were living in a two-dimensional space. That would no doubt complicate their relationships with other people. Try to kiss someone or say something in a 2-D space! Everything is flat! I refer the reader to *Flatland*, Edwin Abbott's novella from 1884, in which a square dreams about a sphere and longs to live in a three-dimensional world, but the authorities see its audacity as pathological (Abbott, 1992).

DOI: 10.4324/9781003221487-10

William Thurston and Jeffrey Weeks, two mathematicians interested in irregular spaces, described what they imagined it would be like to live in the so-called non-orientable space. In this space, there is no inside or outside, no above and below, which means that your right side and your left side are continuous. In an article for the popular French magazine *Pour la science*, they write:

> In such a space, the light emitted by the posterior half of your body penetrates the wall behind you and reappears through the wall in front of you. By looking straight ahead, you can therefore observe your back; look to the right and you will see you left profile; look under your feet and you will see the top of your head.
> (Thurston & Weeks, 1984)

Anyone can have this kind of perceptive experience in a nightmare; however, for some people the experience is permanent. A child in a session with Meltzer drew a castle and said: "When you enter by the front door, you immediately come out the back door ... of another building." There are many pedagogical tools to demonstrate the everyday experience of the blind or the disabled. We should think of something along the lines of "Spend a day as an autistic person!"

Trying to imagine the space inhabited by the so-called autists is of course more complicated than trying to retrain them, like little dogs, to adapt to the rules of our own shared space. Among the professionals, the debate continues: what should be our approach to autism? Should it be psychoanalysis? CBT? Aspirin? Let's try topology!

Alan Turing, like you and me

Have you heard of Alan Turing? Born in London in 1912, he too was seen as odd and mocked by his classmates, but was noticed by his mathematics professors at Cambridge and later became the founder of modern computer science. During World War II, the young Turing was recruited by the British secret services to help them decipher the German army's communications. The Nazis were using the famous Enigma, a supposedly uncrackable coding machine. Turing not only managed to crack its code – and thus change the course of the war – but used it to invent the first modern computer.

Our personal computers have since become much more powerful, but their principle, designed by Turing, remains the same: executing a sequence of tasks by printed circuit boards, which contain information encoded in strings of 0s and 1s, physically represented by the absence or presence of the electric current. Other complex electromechanical machines had of course been built before Turing, such as the Enigma, which was composed of a typewriter keyboard and a rotor mechanism capable of transforming a message into an unreadable series of letters. However, these machines required mechanical actions directed by human operators. Turing was the first to think about writing an algorithm: the first computer programme, a series of tasks and decisions that the machine would execute depending on the context, on the information it received. This programme, which was imprinted on a punch card, could then be "read" by the machine.

While London was suffering under the V2 raids, the British were still unable to decipher the transmissions of the Germans, who kept changing the Enigma codes every day. Turing had the genius idea, which might appear quite simple today: to defeat a machine, you have to build another, more intelligent, and faster machine. He wrote a programme which enabled it to compose all the possible combinations of the intercepted messages, by excluding all the improbable words and only keeping those most likely. And voilà – this ancestor of our computers started spitting out German words, sequences, and phrases, the coordinates of the German bombings.

Today there are codes everywhere and for everything: from frozen meals to psychiatric categories. That doesn't leave much space for the subject! We have more and more communication but less and less speaking. As Lacan used to say, science forecloses the subject. If you don't have the entry code to a building, you have to stay outside. And if your case isn't registered by the Job Centre or the UCAS algorithm, your wishes will simply be ignored.

We all continue struggling with the ghost of Enigma, with our beautiful apps on our glowing smartphones, while regularly forgetting our PINs. In our time, Turing would have been labelled with Asperger's, i.e. considered a high-functioning autistic, or F84.5 in the CIM-10.

We are all F84.5

It is a very interesting question: what changes does the increasing digitalisation of our world induce in us, speaking beings? This question requires us to clarify the difference between human speech and the types of communication used by bees, computers, and HR managers.

Each major technological invention modifies man's relationship to himself, to others, to thought, desire, and time. The arrival of the printing press changed the way we think. Just how radically and permanently will the internet change human thought and language is not quite clear yet. We can observe some local changes, induced by the use of new communication tools, but we do not yet know if these are situational or whether they will become structural. A fairly simple example: a woman is telling me about her recent conversation with her husband: "I told him... and so he said..." Their exchange quickly spirals out of control. When I ask her whether this was indeed a spoken dialogue, she says: "Well, yes... via text." The differentiation between these two actions, writing and speaking, has faded due to the use of instant messaging and emails, which might be helpful in some exchanges but are likely to complicate many others, where the *saying* – the tone – is essential to understanding what is said. Emojis are not always enough.

Digitisation means transforming information into sequences of 0s and 1s, the basis of machine language (for example, the letter A is transcribed as 01000001). This necessarily introduces binary into all aspects of human life. Obviously, it did not take computers to complicate human relationships through binary reasoning, but machine language has greatly accentuated this trend. Better communication is presented as a form of well-being, yet more communication and planning, more programming also means less space for speaking, for the singular, for desire and surprise. Yesterday we were born into a bath of language: today, are we submerged in a bath of algorithms? The generalised use of these programmes already prioritises what linguistics calls the language *code* – in other words, its conventions – while leaving less space for the singular creativity of speaking.

More intelligent, super-computing, and better communicators – but less comfortable with direct speech: with our smartphones and tablets in hand, we have all become a kind of high-functioning autists. People like Elon Musk or the French scientist Laurent Alexandre, who have voiced concerns about the place of artificial intelligence in our lives, believe that there is only one way of making sure we stay in the race: implanting microprocessors in our brains, in order to have access to the kinds of memory and computational power equal to our computers.

Stop calling me Asperger

Johann Hans Karl Asperger was born in 1906 in Vienna. Having graduated with a medical degree in 1932, he became a psychiatrist with a particular interest in autistic children. After his death, a certain type of autism was named after him. Asperger's syndrome is characterised by a tendency to isolate oneself socially and only seek short-term contact with others, as well as by an obsession with technical and scientific problems, often with a passion for complex calculations.

It so happens that a historian has recently shown that Hans Asperger was a highly active participant in the *Aktion T4* scheme, a programme of elimination of children considered unsuitable by the Third Reich ideologists. To be honest, it was not really a shock: we already knew that during the Nazi period, Asperger must have made some concessions, or his career would not have been so stellar. Yet today, things are a bit clearer. Professor Edith Sheffer from Stanford University has carried out extensive research in the Vienna hospital archives and recently published a book, *Asperger's Children: The Origins of Autism in Nazi Vienna*, which documents Asperger's diligent participation in the selection of children to be executed as non-Aryan (Sheffer, 2018). From the paediatric service at the Steinhof Hospital where he practised, Asperger sent these children directly to the infamous Am Spiegelgrund

Clinic, where his colleague Dr Heinrich Gross would experiment on them before killing them. Dr Gross continued his brilliant career until the 1980s.

Beyond the revelations about Asperger's activities, Sheffer's book provoked a reaction among all those who consider themselves autism experts, by showing that the notions underpinning the said syndrome and many others in the field of autism have emerged from this ideological context, of separating high-performing from under-performing children. Of course, today's "abnormal" children are no longer killed – we simply subject them to re-education, in order to make them speak the way they should, to have the right social skills, and not to rock back-and-forth too much.

Thus, all of those who today identify with the little superhumans that children with Asperger's supposedly are must necessarily also feel a sense of unease. It took Sheffer's book for them to begin to ask why they had so readily embraced this nosographic label in the first place. Simon Baron-Cohen, Past-President of the International Society for Autism Research, has recently declared that he no longer "feels comfortable with naming the diagnosis after Hans Asperger". However, he should listen to himself more closely when he says that it might be necessary to change the name and create new *subtypes* (Baron-Cohen, 2018). Since the publication of Sheffer's work, certain groups of Asperger patients have also been campaigning to change the syndrome's name, after having previously campaigned for its recognition. One of these petitions has suggested it should be amended to Social Communication Disorder.

It is often pointed out that the number of diagnosed cases of autism is constantly growing. Is this perhaps because we have been mass-producing them, since Turing invented the computer and its algorithms in the image of his own relationship to the Other, his relationship to the signifier, and since psychologists have come to believe that the human brain functioned like a computer? With our smartphones in hand, we have all become computer-assisted Aspergers.

References

Abbot, E. (1992). *Flatland: A Romance of Many Dimensions*. Mineola, NYC: Dover Thrift.
Baron-Cohen, S. (2018). The truth about Hans Asperger's Nazi collusion. *Nature.com*, 8 May 2018. Retrieved on 1 July 2019 from www.nature.com/articles/d41586-018-05112-1.
Meyronnis, F. (2012). *Tout autre. Une confession*. Paris: Gallimard.
Sheffer, E. (2018). *Asperger's Children: The Origins of Autism in Nazi Vienna*. New York: W.W. Norton.
Thurston, W. & Weeks, J. (1984). Les variétés à trois dimensions. *Pour la Science*, 83.

Afterword
What is the place of psychoanalysis in the treatment of autism today?

In this book, our goal was to present a wide range of psychoanalytic authors offering a Lacanian critique of the mainstream models of treatment and the strictly neuro-developmental conception currently professed as the scientific truth about autism. The question of the aetiology of autism is discussed by most of these thinkers, albeit to a varying degree. What all of them reject is neither the behaviourist, cognitivist, or neuroscientific research as such, nor the question of diagnosis or indeed the political struggle of autists to achieve recognition, but rather the reductive and scientifically dubious "monism", as Jean-Pierre Drapier puts it, the ideology of a purely organic aetiology of autism, its definition as a neuro-developmental disorder. Yet despite all the research carried out so far, no genuine "cause" of autism (organic, genetic, or, for that matter, psychogenic) has been established and given our current state of knowledge, it is impossible to base the diagnosis of autism on any kind of medical imaging or biological analysis. The diagnostic process in which, paradoxically, relational "intuitions" of various actors in a child's life are converted into "scientific" data is aptly described by Pierre-Henri Castel:

> The formalised tests then appear as a way of refining this intuitive judgement and, most importantly, aligning the clinical picture with a pre-constructed medico-social category that gives access to welfare rights, for example to specialised education and benefits, without any certainty that an objective pathological entity has been identified.
>
> (p. 108)

At the same time, the cognitivist and behavioural methods discussed in these texts (ABA, TEACCH, PECS…) are ostensibly not concerned with the psychic functioning of individual children, with their affective life: instead they present a standard of development which individuals are asked to reach, by following a method supposedly generalisable to all.

> The "difficult" behaviour of the child is not questioned and is not understood as a mode of communication or as a result of a specific

difficulty. The child is essentially asked to obey: the risk taken is of a learning to submit which hinders access to independence.

(Maleval, 2010, p. 238)

And even those methods that try to build communication channels by relying on the specificities of the autists' cognitive functioning continue to focus on modifying specific target behaviours and cannot do without resorting to the system of rewards and punishments.

Instead, despite their at-times significant divergences, Lacanian authors see autism first and foremost as a *subjective position*. Rather than seeking to repair or correct an organic deficiency or dysfunction, psychoanalysis approaches each autistic person as a subject in language (although not in discourse and even though his own access to speech may be minimal), irreducible to his biological dimension, with a singular mode of jouissance and having to use various strategies to actively maintain a liveable distance vis-a vis the surrounding world, its objects and the other. Most Lacanian psychoanalysts locate the origins of the autistic defence on the brink of the first of the two stages identified by Lacan as the birth of the human subject: the moment of alienation. "The autist seems to refuse becoming alienated in the Other's language. Muteness, insofar as it means not giving in to the jouissance of the object-voice, is the most radical form of this refusal" (Prieto, p. 48).

Autism is thus a position of rejecting the Other's signifiers *en masse* – in this sense, the Other as the treasure trove of signifiers which can mark the body in a signifying way never comes into existence. The subject cannot be represented by the signifier. What remains is a very real, invasive Other, whose every demand is perceived as intrusive and whose presence constantly has to be kept at bay, as the autistic subject can only realise, in the real, the presence of this Other's fantasmatic object (Di Ciaccia, 2005, p. 107–118). Whether this subject can indeed become a subject of desire, a desiring subject, is a question each time, with each autistic patient. However, as Leonardo Rodriguez writes,

> We must at least be prepared to accept that the autistic subject might be a subject of the unconscious, even if this formula needs to be qualified for every case. If we rule out the possibility that the patient be capable of desiring, then the direction that we impose to the treatment will restrict our field of operations, and we may end up excluding the signs of the patient's desire on the basis of a false premise.
>
> (Rodriguez, p. 26)

Also, he argues, the fact that this desiring subject is largely absent at the beginning of the treatment is not necessarily unique to autism.

The same respect for the singularity of the subject applies to the psychoanalytic approach to *autistic symptoms*. As a symptom in its own right, it is a subjective production. The different behaviours "typical" of autism are discussed by our authors as primarily strategies of defence: creating a boundary or identifying with an object-double which itself can be inserted between the self and the Other. This is the case even with symptoms that the people around autists may find deeply problematic. "A decisive step is taken," Jean-Claude Maleval writes,

> when the study of autism is no longer limited to its cognitive style but seeks to take into account the specificity of his affectivity and jouissance. His irrational behaviours then take on a role: they are appropriate modes of defence against anxiety. Immutability is an attempt to establish proper rules in a disturbing chaotic world, the autistic object is a reassuring protection, which can even serve as a double dynamic if we allow the subject to be supported by it, the treatment of language is done by keeping it away from this particularly distressing object that is the voice, etc.
> (Maleval, 2010, p. 241)

We have seen that stereotypies are the solutions the subject has found to manage a body that he finds indomitable, to place a limit on it, to bring some order into the strange sensations coming from this body, which he doesn't own and which appear inexplicable and impossible to locate. In order to convince the subject to abandon such behaviours, we must first give him the chance to build something that replaces them – simply obliging him to stop this or that behaviour that might be vital for him is an act of unjustifiable cruelty.

If we simply encourage an autistic child to undergo intensive pre-established programmes, we will not get any closer to his complicated relationship to speech and language; if we do not consider what might be at stake for a subject in his repetitive actions or strange behaviours, we cannot understand anything about the terrible anxiety speech provokes in them. For each child, accessing speech is a process. For the subject with autism, language remains too real: the absence of the symbolic operation never rids speech of its excess of jouissance, which can feel mortifying. Some children never talk; others may say the occasional word or make themselves understood by repeating expressions they have heard and can handle more or less successfully (often rote expressions lacking the personal dimension: bits of discourse, advertising slogans). In any case, each example testifies to the fact that talking comes from a deep and intimate place. As clinicians, we try to emphasise to the autistic child that speech is not used exclusively to communicate something, but to seek and obtain a response from the person we are addressing. In other words, to speak is to enter into a dialogue. For the child with autism, talking may mean to have to burst his "bubble" – and this is not always feasible.

Likewise, for the autist, objects do not have exchange value but only use value (i.e. the very particular satisfaction they procure), and are thus not readily interchangeable. The autistic relationship with the object does not pass through the relationship with the other; instead it has the function of a kind of "suitcase", allowing for a localisation of a certain satisfaction. It exists in a continuity with the body, which means that separating oneself from one's objects of satisfaction or interest is difficult if not impossible. In children, this also has consequences for play: the object does not represent the child the way it would in a non-autistic playing; it is not an intermediary, but something that preserves a certain homeostasis.

It is important to understand that the highly specific object of the subject's interest is in itself a therapeutic attempt, that it works as a supplement and that as therapists, we must learn from this solution. For example, an object can serve to mark, to order time or space, turning an unbearable crossing into a more or less comfortable movement. An object brought to the session by an autistic child can help make a strange space look almost familiar, creating a much-needed sense of continuity of time and space. It can be a child's way of bringing order into a chaotic world. It can mitigate the threat of the unexpected, create a bearable way of coexisting with others, of finding a place in the world. The child's apparent "obsessions" or fixations can also have this objective – to bring in a bit of order, to regulate an excess. For these children, the bond with others and with the symbolic world around them is very fragile. Its instability is itself a defence: of a subject with few resources to become a self, faced with a world that cannot be ordered by language. In these ways, the autist tries to include the Other, the others around him and the symbolic organisation that constitutes the natural habitat of speaking beings. For some, these efforts are more successful than for others. The more pacifying the Other, the easier it will be for the subject to be included in the social link.

Being with

The psychoanalytic work with autistic children shows that these children do not always exclude the presence of a working partner, or even that they may seek it, if we know how to respect this necessity, how to listen carefully and talk to them in a way that is not invasive. In all cases, it is about capturing the subtle ways in which the child allows the analyst to stand by his side. If interventions are started early, they can sometimes radically modify the course of events; on the other hand, these authors agree that there is no need to idealise the process and in the day-to-day practice with patients who are sometimes incredibly difficult to communicate with, the very requirement of the "supposition of a subject" may present the psychoanalyst's "boldest challenge", as Jacques Hochmann puts it in his essay.

The way we treat autism allows us to understand more clearly that solutions are always unique and that the child must be accompanied in his work of invention, beyond social ideals and pre-established norms. To force a child into "normality" is to forget that a subject can never be restricted to the opposition between normal and pathological. Each subject and each treatment path are unique. When we respect the inventiveness and the specific interests of each child, we may indeed be able to approach them, helping each subject find his unique solutions among the thousand and one ways of living in the world.

Hence, therapeutic work cannot consist in tearing them away from what already serves as a support, but rather in using this "crutch" to include the child in a relationship with others. The extremely delicate work of the treatment therefore aims, for example, at bringing the autistic object to enter the chain of exchange, to have a place not only in the subject's life but also in his relationship with the world. This can only be achieved if we respect the subject's use of it in the first place. The therapist must find out how to help the subject so that a small object the autist makes use of (perhaps insignificant to a layperson) can be displaced and converted into something else, more compatible with the social bond.

Iván Ruiz and Neus Carbonell write:

> If we work with an autistic subject teaching him to use an instrument the way we believe it should be done, to identify shapes and colours, to repeat "good morning" when entering a room and giving him many other instructions, we will have ignored his discomfort and avoided the question about his subjective involvement in his distress. And perhaps we will have made it a bit more difficult for him to come out of his bubble. The autistic subject must be educated like any other subject; however, it is necessary to distinguish between treatment and pedagogy.

The treatment is essentially aimed at helping the subject be less overwhelmed by anxiety, by the suffering imposed on him by his autistic position, at what prevents him from being in the world with the dignity and respect every human being deserves. This type of progress is therefore hardly measurable in terms of statistics – the number of times that a subject manages to say "good morning" on entering a room tells us nothing about how well he is able to deal with anxiety. The psychoanalytic engagement with autism is not normative – it does not aim at suppressing or ridding the autist of his autism, even though some authors, such as Marie-Christine Laznik (see below), believe that an early intervention may prevent its development. Contrary to the educational approaches, it does not rely on the knowledge of the educator as a form of mastery or expertise, which seems to be the common denominator of the wide range of methods used today. For psychoanalysis, the source of the change is located on the side of the autistic subject and "it is a question of stimulating and accompanying a dynamic of change inherent in the child" (Maleval, 2010, p. 242). Several authors point out that from the accounts of autists who have achieved a high level of autonomy we learned that they have rarely greatly benefited from educational methods alone and often reject them directly; what was important for them was instead to find a space where their own original solutions could be elaborated.

In this book, we have presented perspectives from authors of the Lacanian orientation whose work makes it patently clear that psychoanalysis does have a place in caring for autistic people, despite the socio-historical tensions of its complex history and the amount of media and public scrutiny it has faced in recent years, in France and elsewhere.[1] As we have seen, these authors do not argue for a "purist" approach: the types of treatments described in these accounts are not traditional psychoanalytic cures based on interpretation. Indeed, they cannot be – the difficulty already begins with the fact that the subject we are dealing with does not necessarily pose any demand, though a demand may come from those around him. There is no subject supposed to know. Instead, these treatments emphasise a relational approach, starting from the signs of interest shown by the child and trying to invent a suitable mode of action. "The very idea of interpreting an autistic symptom the way Freud interpreted the hysterical symptom at the beginning of 20th century is utter nonsense, an absurdity", Patrick Landman argues, "and today's analysts work with autists in a completely different way" (Landman, p. 90). These types of applied psychoanalytic interventions, i.e. "applied to the symptom and the form of suffering" (Di Ciaccia, 2005, p. 70) are based on different ways the practitioners have found – and sometimes tried to theorise – of "being with" autistic patients (Drapier's *sideways* presence, Eric Laurent's notion of autism *à deux*), whether it is in an institution or in a consulting room.

Among the numerous initiatives, we would like to highlight three examples of current research and clinical work which seem particularly promising.

The French-Brazilian psychoanalyst and researcher Marie-Christine Laznik, though not represented in this volume, will not be unfamiliar to English-speaking Lacanians: her pioneering work with babies at risk of autism at the Centre Alfred Binet in Paris is well documented and many of her articles have been translated into English. Though Laznik has worked with infants for over 40 years, her approach underwent a significant change after she was introduced to the analyses of home videos carried out by Italian researchers. Here, Laznik understood that the psychogenetic dynamic between babies who were to become autistic and their carers was in fact the very opposite of what certain earlier psychoanalytic authors may have claimed. In other words, rather than seeing cold and incompetent parents whose inadequate care could be blamed for the baby's difficulties, she systematically found that certain babies were less responsive and more withdrawn, and it was this chronic absence of response that gradually eroded the carers' confidence, as well as their competence as parents.

Laznik advocates a multidisciplinary approach to treatment and her team has developed the PREAUT grid, an early-screening tool (Ouss & Laznik et al., 2012). Although she speculates that the specificity of the at-risk babies perhaps lies in their greater sensitivity to emotional cues, i.e. an excess of emotional "empathy", she often repeats that she has strictly "nothing to say" about the aetiology of autism. What she *can* do is clinically identify, as early as at four months of age, those babies in whom the circuit of the drive between the infant and the Other has not been correctly established, leaving the baby in a world of its own.

Following the three stages of the drive described by Freud, the baby (1) reaches towards the oral object (the active phase), then (2) uses this experience to satisfy himself autoerotically by sucking on a thumb etc. (passive phase), and finally (3) must again try to become the object of the other, must try to attract him – a necessary alienation. Laznik describes babies who, from very early on, reach out, search for the other's gaze, offer themselves to the other, offer their foot or another part of their body to be enjoyed in a shared moment of pleasure. This is precisely the kind of behaviour we do not find in babies at risk of autism. This "open" loop of the drive is then what Laznik and her team will endeavour to close through their interventions, as early as possible and always working with both the baby and his parents.

Laznik's singular technique is based on trying to induce and stimulate these shared moments of pleasure, in order to "hook" the baby in and reconnect the drive. In doing so, she makes use of "motherese", the particularly melodious form of prosody used by adults exclusively when speaking to a baby. In these forms of speech, Laznik has identified elements that communicate surprise and pleasure, and which seem able to reach and captivate even very withdrawn babies. In many of the cases, their interventions have proven highly successful.

Another excellent example is the previously mentioned institutional work of *Antenne 110*, which has developed its practice based on the concept of *pratique à pluisiers* ("shared practice"), a term coined by Jacques-Alain Miller. Starting from Lacan's remark (Lacan, 1989) that it is highly problematic for an autistic child to hear the speech of those who are taking care of him, the team have looked for ways of "becoming a partner" to the autistic child, which would enable speech to be heard. This means "situating ourselves as other rather than the fellow human being. An other able to take on the *semblant*, who, while articulating the Other of speech to the Other of language, excludes the excess of jouissance" (Di Ciaccia, 2005, p. 35). These practitioners see their work as conditioned by, on the one hand, the subjective availability of each "partner" to the child's solicitations, and, on the other hand, sharing this responsibility in an exchange with other "partners", who also act "in their own name". Their task is to take up the work already initiated by the child and his singular ways of manipulating his body and objects, in order to "raise them to the dignity of signifiers" – a risky operation offering the child the possibility of effacing the object in order to metaphorise it.

> We start from the child the way he is, with his potentials and incapacities, but also with his privileged object – this can be a stick, a piece of thread, a circuit, Walt Disney, etc. – and we invent different tools and strategies

to extend and shift, expand this special centre of interest and slowly bring the child towards a process of learning. In this way, the child's attention and interest are engaged in the required work, which becomes itself motivating and a source of satisfaction.

(Antenne 110, 2006, p. 27)

Finally, *affinity therapy* is a term originally coined by the journalist Ron Suskind in his book *Life, Animated* (2014), which tells the story of his family's life with his autistic son Owen. In struggling to communicate with the boy, the family comes to embrace his passion for Disney movies, which Owen watches on repeat. These films – repetitive, predictable, with normative plotlines and vivid imagery – give the boy a sense of security. However, their characters and song lyrics also allow him to tackle complex social situations, to take up a position in the world, for example by identifying with the figure of the "side-kick". *Affinity therapy* draws on the experience of individual families and autists, following the child's lead, taking these passions seriously and making use of them in helping him elaborate and invent a way of inscribing himself in the social link. The eponymous collection published by the Research Group on Autism led by Myriam Cherel (Perrin) at the University of Rennes 2 contains a number of similar testimonies of autists, whose passions include horse riding, growing carnivorous plants and Tintin (Perrin, 2015). "Affinity therapy is not a method, but an ethics", says Alexandre Stevens, the founder of *Le Courtil*. An ethics of the singular, which, contrary to "structured learning", offers to become a "partner" to the child, to support the autist in his efforts to construct a space for himself while protecting himself from anxiety, to "be taught by" the autist rather than subjecting them to a process of "retraining".

Again, it is obvious that approaches such as these do not deny the right of autistic children to learning and education – in fact, many of our authors call for a pluralistic approach, a multidisciplinary programme including both psychodynamic and educational methods, in addition to other forms of work such as movement or speech therapy. Others criticise both sides of the current partisan conflicts, which, as Marie-Dominique Amy argues, just deepen the autist's own difficulties by only treating either their cognitive problems *or* their psychic state. "By acting out our divisions, we do nothing but reinforce their own" (Amy, p. 78). In the now plentiful genre of testimonies written by autists themselves, certain accounts suggest that combinations of different approaches have been helpful to them. In his 2012 article in *The Guardian*, where he addresses the controversial French film *The Wall*, the author Henry Bond explains that he has benefited from both CBT and psychoanalysis, which for him addresses philosophical and existential questions going beyond the normative and quantifiable goals and outcomes (Bond, 2012). The fact that other autistic subjects have drawn very little benefit from the psychoanalytic experience is also true – yet, again, we find cases of unfavourable outcomes across all clinical structures. In an interview about her recent book, *Autismes: Comment render les parents fous* (Autisms: How to drive parents mad), which presents clinical vignettes from her practice as well as tracing the endless struggles faced by families of autistic children trying to find suitable forms of treatment, the French analyst and author Catherine Vanier says:

> As psychoanalysts, we cannot guarantee that psychoanalysis alone cures autism. That would be absurd. However, what we can say is that if a child is not considered a small human subject, he will not be alright, even if he is hyper-well trained.
>
> (Vanier, 2014, p. 20)

We are reminded of the work of Françoise Dolto, who, though not primarily conceptually concerned with autism, believed that "a child was a full-fledged person [*une personne à part entière*]". What Dolto was concerned with explicitly was education – supporting children in gaining their autonomy and helping their parents accept this autonomy without anxiety. However, she also argued that for any child, excessive adaptation to educational requirements was in fact a major sign of pathology.

However, these authors do not endorse a kind of naïve eclecticism of treatment or simply call for more coordination of the different approaches. Although all methods of treatment have their successes and failures, *they do not have the same ethical positioning*. While the psychoanalytic setting is flexible, its ethical stance is unique. Lacan's understanding of the analyst's desire as the "desire to obtain pure difference" seems even more pertinent when working with autistic subjects, who, as Rodriguez says, are easily treated as objects by others. Working without preconceptions about the child's journey, without imposing a specific expectation or wish to see something particular, careful not to invade the child's inner world by force yet also respecting the limits imposed by discourse – isn't this what the requirement to limit the Other of jouissance means?

Finally, a number of authors evoke the human dimension of autism and its problems as a magnifying glass on humanity. The questions of otherness, of language as a protection against the hegemony of sameness, are highlighted here in a myriad of singular ways. To conclude, with Rodriguez:

> The lessons that we have gained from the experience with autistic subjects have helped us to learn about human functions that are present in everybody. The marked contrast between autistic and all other subjects in relation to those functions is highly instructive for our understanding of the workings of the unconscious, of language and discourse, of the imaginary and symbolic representation of the body and of affective life – and a few other questions of psychoanalytic interest.

Note

1 In France, this controversy reached a new level in 2013, when the then-minister for the disabled, Marie-Arlette Carlotti, published the *Third Plan for Autism* (2014–2017), which ruled that psychoanalytically oriented institutions working with autistic children would no longer receive public funds.

References

Antenne 110 (2006). Un programme? Pas sans le sujet. *Préliminaire*, 16, 17–41.
Bond, H. (2012). What autism can teach us about psychoanalysis. *Guardian*, 16 April 2012.
Di Ciaccia, A. (2005) La pratique à plusieurs. *La cause freudienne*, 61, 107–118.
Lacan, J. (1989). Geneva lecture on the symptom. *Analysis*, 1, 7–26.
Laznik, M.-C. (2014). Psychoanalytic treatment of a two month old baby with an autistic brother, showing warning signs of a similar development. *Journal of the Centre for Freudian Analysis and Research*, 25, 225–236.
Maleval, J-C. (2010). Quelqu'un qui puisse lâcher prise. In B. de Halleux (Ed.), *Quelque chose à dire à l'enfant autiste*. Paris: Michèle, 237–259.
Ouss, L., Laznik, M.-C.*et al.* (2012). PREAUT grid: a tool to early determine risk of autism among at risk epileptic babies? *Neuropsychiatrie de l Enfance et de l Adolescence* 60(5), S204.
Perrin, M. (Ed.) (2015). *Affinity Therapy. Nouvelles recherches sur l'autisme*. Rennes: Presses Universitaires de Rennes.
Suskind, R. (2014). *Life, Animated: A Story of Sidekicks, Heroes and Autism*. Glendale, CA: Kingswell.
Vanier, C. (2014). Autour d'*Autisme: Comment rendre les parents fous!* de Catherine Vanier. *Figures de la psychanalyse*, 28(2), 21–31.

Index

ABA 2, 9, 20
aetiology 8, 9, 10, 31, 59, 61, 89, 91, 119, 125
Antenne 110 7, 125, 126
antisocial 28, 30
anxiety 1–10, 45–56, 60–71, 94, 97–102, 105, 121–127
approaches 5–10, 11n4, 17, 35, 55, 78–81, 93, 97, 100, 105, 110, 120–127
Asperger, H. 11, 11n1, 14, 24n3, 74, 99, 101, 118
Asperger syndrome 17, 20, 99, 101, 108, 117–118
autistic spectrum 1, 8, 17, 23, 92, 99
autistic subject 2–3, 5, 8, 26–29, 34–37, 39, 49, 51, 56, 66–67, 120, 123

Baio, V. 7
behaviour 1–11, 19–21, 32, 42–43, 53, 55–56, 60, 69–71, 75, 78–86, 89, 92–94, 98, 102, 105, 11, 119; behavioural 112, 119; behaviourism 111–112; behaviourist 87, 89–90, 94–95, 98, 103–107, 111–112, 119–121, 125
behavioural 1,2, 7–9, 11n4, 20, 75, 80, 83, 112, 119; behavioural hypothesis 80
Bertin, M. 2
Bettelheim, B. 2, 112
biological 1, **2**, 3, 5, 10, **42**, **46**, 47, 55, 56, 56, 69, 94, 100, 107, 119–120; biologically 3; neurobiological 16, 104, 112; biological reality 56
Bleuler, E. 5
Body 5, 11n3, 28, 30, 34, 37, 42, 44–45, **47**, 48–50, 53–56, 61, 64, 69, 72–74, 97, 99, 115, 129–121–122, 125, 127; body image 9; social body 20

Bonneuil-sur Marne 6
Borelle, C. 106–113
Bruno, P. 31, 35

Campbell, P. 31
capitalist 1, 56, 100
Carbonell, Camos, N. 2, 4, 10, 102n1, 123
causality 4, 9, 42, 61, 88–89, 92, 109
clinical 2, 5,25–39, 48, 68–70, 72, 91, 99, 102n2, 124, 127; clinical experience 9, 23, 28, 30, **37, 87, 92**; clinical picture 108–109, 119, clinical practice 36; clinical work 8, 25, 33
cognitive 10, 14, 17, 38, 78–79, 82, 85–86, 106–107, 120–121, 126; cognitive approaches 8; cognitive-behavioural 1
communication 1, 7, 11n2, 11n4, 36, 50, 61, 67, 77–79, 81, 84, 89, 97, 101, 115–120
creation 6, 13, 26–27, 37, 62, 77

Dardot, P. 19
desire 6, 10–11, 16, 25, 26, 29, 31, 35, 37–37, 46, 48, 60–61, 66, 77, 82, 90, 92, 94, 99–100, 105, 116–117, 120
Development 4, 9, 13
developmental 1, 2, 10–11
Di Ciaccia, A. 120, 124–125
diagnosis 1, 3, 7–10, 15, 18, 25, 30, 35, 59–60, 62, 89, 96–100, 107, 109–11, 118, 119
discourse, 5, 6, 9, 26–28, 30, 32, 34–49, 42, 47, 49, 50, 60, 63, 64, 71, 94, 100, 120–121, 127
disorder 1, 3, 10, 13–14, 19, 24n4, 25–26, 30, 38, 88–89, 92, 96, 98–102, 107–112, 118, 119

Index

Dolto, F. 127
drive 5, 7, 34–35, 50, 55, 60, 69, 84, 94, 125
drug 1, 3, 44, 56, 100–101, 103
DSM 1, 5, 10, 17, 19, 31–32, 88–89, 100
Durey, B. 20

echolalia 7, 21, 25, 32, 34–39, 48, 50, 72, 97
education 6–7, 9, 11n2, 15, 18–19, 21, 23, 28, 30, 35, 126–127; re-education 3–5, 90, 94; educational 6, 9, 11n2, 16, 19,39, 55–56, 77–80, 90, 92, 94, m123, 126–127; psychoeducational work 84–85
epidemic 1, 62
epistemology 107; epistemological 10, 59, 94, 103, 107
ethical 9, 13, 26, 29, 39, 100, 107, 127

Faulkner, W. 14
Freud, S. 5, 22, 31, 33, 46, 84, 90, 113, 124–125; Freudian 50, 64, 87, 112

genetic 3–4, 13, 16–17, 19, 31, 45, 47, 77, 88, 106, 119R; biogenetic 9, 42; biogeneticists 20; psychogenetic 59, 124
Grandin, T. 27, 52–54, 94

hypothesis **2**, 3, **4**, 10, 33, 42, 80, 93n1, 97, 101–102, 108

identification 8, 15–16, 20, 25, 34, 45, 53, 55, 87
individual 9, 10–11, 15, 17, 19–22, 42–43, 56, 78–80, 82, 84, 90, 93–94, 104–109, 111–113, 119, 126; inter-individual 8, 85; individualised 11n4, 14, 15, 77, 81, 85
Intolerable 34
intrusion 11n4, 28, 34, 55
invention 8, 27, 32, 56. 116, 122
isolation 1, 35, 47, 56, 96–97

jouissance 5, 7, 35, 37, 44, 46–56, 63–66, 69–71, 120–121, 125, 127

Kanner, L. 14, 19, 27, 29, 31–34, 36, 47–48, 53, 72–74
Klein, M. 15, 33, 68, 87

Lacan, J. 5, 9, 25–28, 31, 33–37, 39, 45, 47, 49, 52, 63–66, 97, 116, 120, 125, 127

Laia, S. 5
lalangue 9, 35–36, 46, 68, 70
language 2, 4–5, 7, 9, 11, 26, 30, 32, 34–36, 42, 44, 46–48, 50–51, 56, 59, 61–63, 66, 68–71, 75, 77, 97, 99, 101, 116–117, 120–122, 125, 127; metalanguage 84
Laval, C. 19
Laurent, E. 100, 124
Laznik, M.-C. 35, 123–125
learning **5**, 6, 10, 11n4, 20, 21, 35, 42, 44, 55–56, 60, 78–83, 92, 120, 126
Le Courtil 4, 7, 126
Lefort, R. & R. 5–6, 33–34, 36, 38, 42, 46, 49–51
Lovaas, I. 20, 55, 80

Mahler, M. 15, 33, 59
mainstream 8, 119
Maleval, J.-C. 35–36, 51, 54, 120–121, 123
Malone, K. 6
Mannoni, M. 6
Meltzer, D. 15, 33, 87, 114–115
Miller, J.-A. 27, 125
Mira, V. 30
Misès, M. 15

neoliberal 8, **13**, 18, 20–24, 105
neoliberalism 8, 18, 21–22
neurodiversity 1, 11, 89
neuroplasticity 78, 84
neuroscience 19, 30, 43, 56, 78, 87–88, 106
Nomine,' B. 49

object a 34, 46, 49–50, 63–64, 67; autistic objects 35; object-voice 7, 46, 48, 55–56
Obsessive 1, 53
Other 4–6, 8–9, 29, 34–37, 45–50, 56–57, 61, 96–97, 99, 118, 120–122, 12; Birth of the Other 33; real Other 66, Other's presence 67, 71; Other's signifiers 67–68, 70, 120; *Other voices* 55

PECS 81, 119
Peeters, T. 7
pharmaceutical 1, 3, 42, 100, 101
Pommier, G. 43,45
production 7, 25–26, 29, 32, 35, 56, 63, 65, 68–69, 121

prognosis 68, 97, 107, 109
psychiatry 1, 6, 8, 15–16, 18–19, 24, **30**, 31, 87, 89–91, 94, 100, 103, 105, 107
psychosis 6, 9, 15–17, 19, 26, 42, 44, 47, 50–51, 60, 65–66, 72, 88, 91

real 6, 29, 34, 47, 49, 51, 53, 55, 56, 59–60, 62, **64**–66, 102, 120–121; real desire 29
repetition 2, 8, 32, 35–36, 46–50, 83
repetitive 1, 7, 28, 32, 38, 48, 56, 70, 72, 89, 98, 100, 111, 121
re-education 3–5, 90, 94, 101, 118
repression 27, 46
responsibility 17, 27, 38, 42, 111, 112, 125
Rodriguez, L. 9, *26*, 31, 35, 39, 120, 127
Ruiz, L. 2, 4, 10, *98*, 102n1, 123

schizophrenia 14–15, *19*, 30–31, 35–56, 50–51
Schopler, E. 80
segregation 1, 13, 30, 89
Sellin, B. 8, 27, 104
Sheffer, E. 24n3, 117–118
signifying alienation 9, 63, 69–70
Silvestre, M. 5
sinthome 27, 33, 51–52, 54, 65–66
Singer, J. 11n2
singular 11, 25, 56, 88, 117, 120, 125–127
singularity 3, 9, 26, 39, 55, 120
social skills 1, 2, 111, 118
Soler, C. 35, 64–65
stereotypies 23, 7–8, 97–98, 100–101, 111, 121
Stevens, A. 4, 126
spectrum *see* autistic spectrum
speech 1, 5–6, 11, 15, 25–26, 29, 32, 34, 36–39, 46–48, 55, 60, 66–71, 75, 75n3, 81, 90, 96, 116–117, 120–121, 125–126
stereotypical 29, 38, 42, 60
subjectivity 1, 4, 29–30, 39, 60, 100, 104

surveillance 22–23; surveillance capitalism 2
Suskind, R. 126
symbolic 4, 29–30, 44, 46–48, 51, 55–56, 59, 64–65, 72, 121–122. 127; symbolically 45
symptom 1–2, 6, 9–10, 14–15, 21, 23, 25–26, 33, 37, 43, 46, 60–62, 64–66, 90, 97, 99–101, 110, 112, 120–121, 124; symptomatic 32, 72

Taylor, B. 3
TEACCH 7, 11, 55, 80–81, 85, 103
Tendlarz, S. 8
Therapy 1–2, 7, 13, 23, 48, 60, 71, 75n3, 77, 90–91, 93, 111, 126
traits 11, 25, 60, 96
transference 21, 29, 34, 60, 66–67, 84, 93, 112
treatment 1–3, 5–10, 13–16, 18, 23–27, 29–30, 35–38, 59–60, 64, 66, 74, 75, 75n3, 77–79, 85, 90–93, 96, 101–104, 107, 109, 111–112, 119–121, 123–124, 127–128
Turing, A. 115–116, 118
Tustin, F. 15, 33, 59, 87

Unconscious 16, 26, 30, 37, 62, 64, 120, 127
Universal 25–26, 28, 37, 105

Vanier, C. 45, 127
Voice 17–18, 24, 36–37, 42, 46–48, 50–51, 61, 66–67, 69–70, 72, 90, 99–100, 104, 117, 121; *see* object-voice

Watson, L. 20
Williams, D. 27, 49–50, 56
Winnicott, D. 6

Zuboff, S. 2

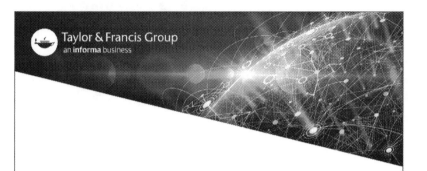

Printed in the United States
by Baker & Taylor Publisher Services